THE CLIMATE CHANGE CRISIS

By Anna Collins

Portions of this book originally appeared in *Global Warming* by Debra A. Miller.

LUCENT PRESS

Published in 2019 by
Lucent Press, an Imprint of Greenhaven Publishing, LLC
353 3rd Avenue
Suite 255
New York, NY 10010

Designer: Seth Hughes
Editor: Jennifer Lombardo

Library of Congress Cataloging-in-Publication Data

Names: Collins, Anna, author.
Title: The climate change crisis / Anna Collins.
Description: New York : Lucent Press, [2019] | Includes bibliographical
  references and index.
Identifiers: LCCN 2017056681| ISBN 9781534563445 (library bound book) | ISBN
  9781534563469 (pbk. book) | ISBN 9781534563452 (e-book)
Subjects: LCSH: Climatic changes–Social aspects. | Climate change mitigation.
Classification: LCC QC903 .C6275 2019 | DDC 304.2/8–dc23
LC record available at https://lccn.loc.gov/2017056681

Printed in the United States of America

CPSIA compliance information: Batch #BS18KL: For further information contact Greenhaven Publishing LLC, New York, New
York at 1-844-317-7404.

Please visit our website, www.greenhavenpublishing.com. For a free color catalog of all our
high-quality books, call toll free 1-844-317-7404 or fax 1-844-317-7405.

CONTENTS

A dolescence is a time when many people begin to take notice of the world around them. News channels, blogs, and talk radio shows are constantly promoting one view or another; very few are unbiased. Young people also hear conflicting information from parents, friends, teachers, and acquaintances. Often, they will hear only one side of an issue or be given flawed information. People who are trying to support a particular viewpoint may cite inaccurate facts and statistics on their blogs, and news programs present many conflicting views of important issues in our society. In a world where it seems everyone has a platform to share their thoughts, it can be difficult to find unbiased, accurate information about important issues.

It is not only facts that are important. In blog posts, in comments on online videos, and on talk shows, people will share opinions that are not necessarily true or false, but can still have a strong impact. For example, many young people struggle with their body image. Seeing or hearing negative comments about particular body types online can have a huge effect on the way someone views himself or herself and may lead to depression and anxiety. Although it is important not to keep information hidden from young people under the guise of protecting them, it is equally important to offer encouragement on issues that affect their mental health.

The titles in the Hot Topics series provide readers with different viewpoints on important issues in today's society. Many of these issues, such as teen pregnancy and Internet safety, are of immediate concern to young people. This series aims to give readers factual context on these crucial topics in a way that lets them form their own opinions. The facts presented throughout also serve to empower readers to help themselves or support people they know who are struggling with many of the challenges adolescents face today. Although negative viewpoints are not ignored or downplayed, this series allows young people to see that the challenges they face are not insurmountable. Eating disorders can be overcome, the Internet can be navigated safely, and pregnant teens do not have to feel hopeless.

Quotes encompassing all viewpoints are presented and cited so readers can trace them back to their original source, verifying for themselves whether the information comes from a reputable place. Additional books and websites are listed, giving readers a starting point from which to continue their own research. Chapter questions encourage discussion, allowing young people to hear and understand their classmates' points of view as they further solidify their own. Full-color photographs and enlightening charts provide a deeper understanding of the topics at hand. All of these features augment the informative text, helping young people understand the world they live in and formulate their own opinions concerning the best way they can improve it.

Ignored for Too Long

Climate change is one of the most pressing environmental issues the world is facing, yet many people continue to deny that it is a real problem. Global warming, which is part of climate change, refers to rising global temperatures caused by high levels of carbon dioxide and other gases in the atmosphere. These are called "greenhouse gases" because they trap heat that would normally escape through the atmosphere, causing the earth to become warmer—much the way a greenhouse that is used for growing plants keeps heat inside. At least some of these greenhouse gases are produced by burning fossil fuels such as oil, natural gas, and coal. Global warming contributes to climate change by, as the term suggests, changing Earth's climate. This includes changes such as rising sea levels, melting glaciers, and unusual weather patterns. Many people use the terms "global warming" and "climate change" interchangeably, which creates some confusion. Scientists make a distinction between the two terms, but news programs and websites sometimes do not.

One of the most vocal climate change activists is former American vice president and presidential candidate Al Gore, who, since his defeat in the 2000 presidential race, has waged a worldwide publicity campaign about the dangers of climate change. Gore's campaign began with speeches and a slide show of compelling photos, graphs, and timelines, and in 2006, Gore unveiled a documentary and book on the topic, both named *An Inconvenient Truth*. In 2017, he released a sequel to this documentary called *An Inconvenient Sequel: Truth to Power*.

An Inconvenient Truth was critically acclaimed and won two Academy Awards in 2007. In the film, Gore uses humor, science, and personal stories to show how human activities that produce carbon dioxide and other greenhouse gases are the cause of the rise in Earth's temperatures. The film claims global

Global warming and climate change affect the entire planet, but not always in the same ways.

warming may already be producing frightening weather, including stronger hurricanes, flooding, and torrential rains for some parts of the world, as well as record heat and drought in other areas. These climate changes, Gore and others warn, could in turn result in numerous other problems—everything from new mosquito-borne disease pandemics to the loss of animal species, such as the polar bear, that cannot adapt quickly enough to the rapid temperature increases.

Also in 2007, Gore won an international award—the Nobel Peace Prize—for his efforts. He shared the award with scientists from the Intergovernmental Panel on Climate Change (IPCC), a United Nations (UN) organization set up to investigate and report on the causes, effects, and solutions to climate change. In his acceptance speech in Oslo, Norway, on December 10, 2007, Gore urged the public and policy makers to act immediately to prevent what could become catastrophic disasters in the future, explaining, "We have the ability to solve this crisis and avoid the worst—though not all—of its consequences, if we act boldly, decisively and quickly."[1]

Former vice president Al Gore, shown here, is one of the most well-known supporters of efforts to stop climate change.

The other recipient of the Nobel Peace Prize, the IPCC, was honored because of a series of scientific reports it has issued over the past several decades, which the Nobel committee said had created a broad consensus about the connection between human activities and global warming. The IPCC's 2007 report, "Mitigation of Climate Change," warned that unless governments acted quickly to reduce global emissions, greenhouse gases could rise by 25 to 90 percent over year-2000 levels by the year 2030. In fact, experts say countries such as the United States would need to reduce emissions of greenhouse gases by at least 80 percent by 2050, and Gore has urged the country to take the lead with a 90 percent reduction in the United States.

Denying the Problem

Although some countries have committed to reducing their emissions, others—including the United States—have not always listened to these warnings. President George W. Bush, for example, began his administration in 2000 by suddenly reversing a campaign promise to regulate U.S. carbon dioxide emissions and by withdrawing the United States from ongoing negotiations on the Kyoto Protocol, an international treaty negotiated in 1997 that set targets for emissions reductions by developed nations. President Barack Obama's administration did not follow in Bush's footsteps; in 2015, the United States joined about 200 other countries in the Paris Agreement, an international treaty that outlined steps governments could take to reduce emissions and stop global warming. Some people applauded this move, but others believed the agreement was not as progressive as it seemed. In 2017, after Donald Trump became president, he indicated that he wanted the United States to pull out of the Paris Agreement. Some people became angry because Trump's administration has enacted many policies that put the environment at further risk; others agreed with Trump that the Paris Agreement was not in the best interests of the country, claiming that the laws the document requires countries to adopt would place a large burden on the economy of the United States. Because of the nature of the agreement, however, it was stated that pulling out could take up to three years. Additionally, as of January 2018, the Trump administration has offered no alternative plans to combat climate change. The president has called it a hoax, or trick, set up by the Chinese to cripple the U.S. economy. There is no proof, however, that this is true.

Addressing climate change, therefore, comes with a unique challenge. With most issues, the biggest obstacle is raising public awareness, but most people have already heard a lot about climate change. Instead, the problem is convincing policy makers as well as a large portion of citizens that climate change is not only real but also a significant problem. Many people believe taking measures to fight climate change will have no effect on the environment and will hurt the economy. In truth, according to many experts, the effort is both necessary and worthwhile. If people continue to ignore climate change, the earth may soon become unlivable for humans and many other species. Tackling the problem head-on will open up jobs in new industries, create a more stable and healthy environment, and ensure that life survives on Earth for decades to come.

CHAPTER 1

Understanding Climate Change

Although some people believe climate change is a myth, there is much scientific evidence to show that it exists. According to researchers, if no effort is made to reduce the temperature of the planet, climate change will soon become irreversible. They warn that if this happens, the planet is likely to become unlivable for humans and most animals. Weather changes would affect food, housing, and transportation, and certain areas may get too hot for people to live in at all.

Earth's Natural Changes

Climate scientists have known since the 18th century that Earth's climate can change—sometimes dramatically—due to natural causes. In fact, evidence from ice cores extracted from the Arctic and Antarctic regions show that planetary temperatures have varied by up to 18 degrees Fahrenheit (10 degrees Celsius) during the last 350,000 years. Long periods of lower temperatures have resulted in prolonged ice ages that lasted tens of thousands of years. Scientists know of at least five ice ages in the Earth's history but suspect there may have been more. About 18,000 years ago, during the last ice age—officially called the Pleistocene Ice Age, but often known in popular culture as just "the ice age"—massive glaciers up to 12,000 feet (3,657.6 m) thick covered almost one-third of the earth's land surface, including much of North America, Europe, and Asia. Areas not covered by glaciers were largely cold and desolate deserts that supported only very hardy plant and animal life, and sea levels dropped more than 400 feet (122 m).

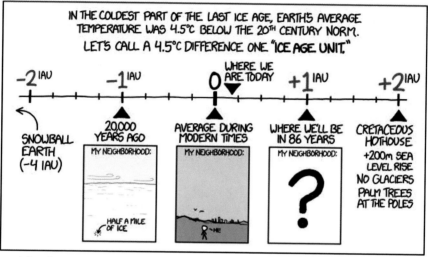

WITHOUT PROMPT, AGGRESSIVE LIMITS ON CO_2 EMISSIONS, THE EARTH WILL LIKELY WARM BY AN AVERAGE OF 4°-5°C BY THE CENTURY'S END.

HOW BIG A CHANGE IS THAT?

IN THE COLDEST PART OF THE LAST ICE AGE, EARTH'S AVERAGE TEMPERATURE WAS 4.5°C BELOW THE 20TH CENTURY NORM. LET'S CALL A 4.5°C DIFFERENCE ONE "ICE AGE UNIT."

-2 IAU   -1 IAU   0 WHERE WE ARE TODAY   +1 IAU   +2 IAU

SNOWBALL EARTH (-4 IAU)

20,000 YEARS AGO
MY NEIGHBORHOOD:
HALF A MILE OF ICE

AVERAGE DURING MODERN TIMES
MY NEIGHBORHOOD:

WHERE WE'LL BE IN 86 YEARS
MY NEIGHBORHOOD:
?

CRETACEOUS HOTHOUSE
+200m SEA LEVEL RISE
NO GLACIERS
PALM TREES AT THE POLES

A few degrees may not seem like much, but they can make a big difference, as this installment of the webcomic xkcd shows.

Some climate changes have been sudden, and they appear to have caused mass extinctions of large numbers of the planet's animal and plant species. The end of the dinosaur era, for example, coincided with a sudden global cooling that was likely caused by an enormous asteroid colliding with the earth. Scientists believe the asteroid caused dirt and other debris to be thrown into the atmosphere, blocking sunlight and cooling the planet. About 11,720 years ago, however, the earth began experiencing an interglacial period that has been more stable than any other period, with no major climate fluctuations. Cold deserts and glaciers have given way to flowering forests, grasslands, and an abundance of plant and animal species, and the human population has soared under these conditions. This era, known as the Holocene Period, is the time humanity is currently living in.

Within these larger climate fluctuations, smaller-scale warming and cooling cycles have historically occurred. For instance, a period known as the Younger Dryas occurred between the

Pleistocene Ice Age and the Holocene Period. The earth began warming up as the ice age ended, then quickly shifted back to extremely cold conditions. Some experts believe this is because when the warming temperatures caused the ice sheets to start melting, the meltwater ran into the ocean and cooled it down, which led to changes in ocean circulation, salinity (amount of salt), and other factors that affected the overall temperature. When the amount of meltwater decreased, the earth warmed up again and stayed relatively stable.

However, this does not mean today's climate never changes. Natural changes are fueled by a number of forces—such as volcanic activity, cloud cover, the changing intensity of the sun's radiation, and varying ocean currents and temperatures—that have caused fluctuations in temperatures during the last 1,000 years. During the Medieval Warm Period, for example, which lasted from approximately AD 900 to 1300, temperatures were warm and comfortable for humans. From around 1300 to about 1870, however, the earth experienced what has been called the Little Ice Age. During this period, the average temperatures were about 1.1 degrees Fahrenheit (0.6 degrees Celsius) colder than they previously had been. In some places, this resulted in harsher winters, shorter growing seasons, a wetter climate, crop failures, and other problems, which *Encyclopedia Britannica* described:

> *Alpine glaciers advanced far below their previous (and present) limits, obliterating farms, churches, and villages in Switzerland, France, and elsewhere. Frequent cold winters and cool, wet summers led to crop failures and famines over much of northern and central Europe. In addition, the North Atlantic cod fisheries declined as ocean temperatures fell in the 17th century ...*

> *Norse colonies in Greenland were cut off from the rest of Norse civilization; the western colony of Greenland collapsed through starvation, and the eastern colony was abandoned.*[2]

The effects of some of these problems were not immediately obvious, and in some cases, social factors also played a role in making the problems worse. For instance, between 1845 and 1852, a potato famine occurred in Ireland, killing the majority of the potato crop. According to *Encyclopedia Britannica,* potatoes were the main source of food for nearly half the Irish population; poorer people could not afford most other foods, so they relied heavily on their potato crops to feed them. The government's failure to provide aid to its people reduced the Irish population by about 25 percent in just six years. The cause of the famine was a mold called *Phytophthora infestans,* which was accidentally brought from North America to Ireland. However, its effects might not have been so devastating if Ireland had not had unusually cool, moist weather that year, allowing the mold to flourish and rot the fields of potatoes.

The Irish Potato Famine was caused by environmental factors but was made worse by social factors.

The Little Ice Age was not caused by humans; researchers believe a decrease in the sun's intensity, changes in the atmosphere, and volcanic explosions that increased the amount of sunlight-blocking ash and dust in the air contributed to the lower temperatures, and over time, these issues resolved themselves. However, it shows what an enormous effect even small changes in temperature can have on the current way of life for many societies.

A Protective Layer

Scientists say Earth's temperatures are largely determined by the balance between the amount of sun energy entering the atmosphere and the amount of energy lost from the earth into space. One of the most important climate mechanisms affecting this balance is a natural greenhouse effect—a band of gases that trap the heat coming from the planet's surface similar to the way a greenhouse warms the air inside its glass walls during a cold winter. These gases include water vapor, methane, nitrous oxide, chlorofluorocarbons, and carbon dioxide.

These greenhouse gases allow visible sunlight energy to penetrate deep into the atmosphere, where much of it is absorbed by the oceans and land masses. When this stored energy is released back toward space as infrared radiation, or heat, the greenhouse gases then act as an insulating blanket, absorbing and holding the heat in the lower atmosphere and helping to maintain the warm temperatures needed for humans to survive. According to the National Aeronautics and Space Administration (NASA), the average overall temperature for the earth as of 2018 is 59 degrees Fahrenheit (15 degrees Celsius), thanks to these gases. As climate expert Mayer Hillman explained, "Without this natural greenhouse effect, the planet would be over 35°F cooler than it is now—too cold for us to inhabit."[3]

People who study climate change often study glaciers. Because ice is white, glaciers such as the one shown here reflect sunlight rather than absorbing it.

The amount of heat trapped in this greenhouse process, however, varies depending on a number of factors. Some sunlight never reaches the earth's surface because it is reflected back into space by clouds and various types of particles and pollutants in the air. In addition, different regions on the planet's surface reflect and absorb solar radiation differently. The ice caps at each of the earth's poles, for example, act as giant mirrors that reflect back most of the sunlight that hits them, while exposed desert soils, oceans, and forested areas tend to absorb more of the sun's energy, helping to heat the atmosphere. A third factor is the concentration of greenhouse gases in the atmosphere, with higher levels producing more warming. All of these elements must be in balance to produce average global temperatures that are in the relatively narrow range necessary for humans, plants, and animals to survive on the planet's fragile surface, seas, and skies.

"THE SINGLE GREATEST THREAT"

"Climate change ... is the single greatest threat that societies face today."

—James Gustave Speth, environmentalist and law professor at Vermont Law School

James Gustave Speth, "The Single Greatest Threat," *Harvard International Review*, June 21, 2007. hir.harvard.edu/article/?a=1346.

The Human Effect

Until recently, humans did not significantly affect the much larger forces of climate and atmosphere. Many scientists believe, however, that with the dawn of the industrial age—and the burning of fossil fuels such as coal, natural gas, and oil that are formed from the decomposed remains of prehistoric plants and animals—humans began to significantly add to the amounts of carbon dioxide and other greenhouse gases in the atmosphere, enhancing the planet's natural greenhouse effect and causing higher temperatures.

The Industrial Revolution began in the late 18th and early 19th centuries in Great Britain, when manual labor began to be replaced by machinery fueled by new sources of energy. The first sign of this change was mechanization of England's textile, or fabric, mills, the development of iron-making techniques, and the increasing use of coal rather than wood and waterpower for heating, industry, and transportation. Around 1850, steam power was invented as a way to use coal energy more efficiently, and soon, steam engines were used to power trains, ships, and industrial machinery of all sorts. These inventions spread throughout Europe, the United States, and other regions, bringing enormous changes in society and commerce. Later in the 19th century, scientists learned how to generate electricity, and the discovery of oil led to the invention of the internal combustion engine, which is the type of engine that powers a car. Both of these technological developments further changed the way humans lived and worked around the globe.

By the end of the 20th century, the world was completely dependent on and rapidly depleting the planet's fossil fuels. As Hillman explained, "Fossil fuels contain the energy stored from the sun that took hundreds of thousands of years to accumulate, yet within the space of a few generations—a mere blink of the planet's life so far—we are burning it."[4]

The result of this rapid burning of fossil resources, many scientists believe, is rising concentrations of greenhouse gases that may be overheating the planet. Scientists have determined, for example, that concentrations of carbon dioxide have been increasing since the beginning of the Industrial Revolution, when coal was burned in large amounts. This created visible pollution in England, especially London; a thick cloud of smog constantly hung over the city. Author Bill Bryson described its effects:

> So hard was it to find one's way that people not infrequently walked into walls or tumbled into unseen voids. In one famous incident, seven people in a row fell into the [River] Thames, one after the other. In 1854, when Joseph Paxton suggested building an eleven-mile-long "Grand Girdle Railway" to link all the principal railway termini in London, he proposed to build it under glass so that passengers would be insulated from London's unwholesome air. It was more desirable evidently to be inside with the thick smoke of trains than outside with the thick smoke of everything else.[5]

The Industrial Revolution changed how goods were made, how people lived, and how people affected the climate.

The invention of electricity and the use of oil instead of coal lessened the smog but did not eliminate pollution; it became largely invisible but still measurable. In 1750, there were 280 parts per million (ppm) of carbon dioxide in the atmosphere, but by 2005, the levels of carbon dioxide had risen to 380 ppm, an increase of more than one-third. Much of this increase has occurred since 1959 as world energy usage has expanded dramatically. As of 2015, which is the latest global data available as of early 2018, China was responsible for most of the world's greenhouse gas emissions, and the United States was the second-largest emitter. Although each Chinese individual is responsible for a lower level of emissions than American individuals—in 2015, China's per capita (individual) emissions rate was 7.26 tons (6.59 mt) of carbon dioxide, compared to 17.11 tons (15.53 mt) for the United States—China has a higher emissions rate overall because its population is so much greater than that of other countries. Other countries with high emissions include members of the European Union, while the lowest emissions come from various nations in Africa and the Caribbean.

The major source of human-produced greenhouse emissions in every country is the use of fossil fuels to create energy. This includes things such as transportation, home heating, and electricity generation. In 2013, the energy sector accounted for 72 percent of global emissions. Cutting down forests, which absorb carbon dioxide, to make way for human developments and converting woodlands, grasslands, and prairies into farmland for agriculture also allows more greenhouse emissions to stay in the atmosphere.

Studying Climate Change

Scientists had long suspected a link between industrialization and global warming, but serious study of the issue did not begin until the second half of the 20th century. In 1895, Swedish scientist Svante Arrhenius was the first to suggest that the burning of fossil fuels adds carbon dioxide gas to the earth's atmosphere and could raise the planet's average temperature. He also suggested that this would produce other negative climate changes. At the time and for decades thereafter, however, Arrhenius's discovery of the greenhouse effect was dismissed by the main-stream scientific community, which reasoned that such a major climate change would not likely be produced by humans and could only happen slowly over tens of thousands of years. Most scientists at the time also believed the oceans would absorb most of the carbon dioxide humans produced.

By the 1960s, however, scientists began to take what Arrhenius had said seriously. Improved instruments for measuring longwave radiation—which includes infrared radiation—allowed them to prove that Arrhenius's theory was correct, and studies also confirmed that carbon dioxide levels were rising every year. In 1958, Charles D. Keeling, a scientist with the Scripps Institute of Oceanography in California, conducted the first reliable measurements of atmospheric carbon dioxide at the Mauna Loa Observatory in Hawai'i and found concentrations of the gas to be 310 ppm and growing.

Over the next several decades, scientists used a variety of methods to study exactly how the Earth's temperature was changing. Some scientists studied paleoclimatic data, which includes ancient tree rings, corals, fossils, pollens, sediment cores, ice cores, and cave stalactites. This data allowed them to compare ancient temperatures with modern data as well as examine global temperature fluctuations over the last several centuries and even farther back in time. Other researchers invented mathematical models of the climate, which allowed for predictions to be made about temperature changes when the amount of carbon dioxide input was

Svante Arrhenius, shown here, was the first scientist to study humanity's effect on global warming and climate change.

THE ELECTROMAGNETIC SPECTRUM

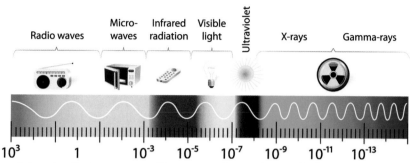

Infrared radiation is a type of longwave radiation that can be felt as heat. When scientists developed instruments to measure longwave radiation more accurately, they were able to prove that global temperatures were indeed rising.

increased. In recent decades, these climate models have been greatly improved by the use of computers, which can incorporate massive amounts of weather information into the climate formulas and produce much more accurate predictions of future climate changes. Also during the last 30 years, scientists began to use satellites to observe the earth's changing climate. All the methods of climate change research have some scientific uncertainties, but each suggests that the earth has warmed over the last 100 years and that it is likely to grow even warmer if something is not done to lower the current rate of global emissions. Today, at least 97 percent of climate scientists agree that human activity has played a huge part in climate change.

Slow to Understand

Despite these scientific findings, however, there was considerable disagreement within the scientific community about global warming throughout the 1980s and 1990s. Many scientists accepted that a warming trend was likely but believed that average temperatures would rise only a few degrees in the next century—not a significant change that seemed to require immediate policy changes. In addition, a number of scientists were equally concerned about the effects of smog, which they feared could potentially block sunlight and cause the world to cool too much rather than heat up. In fact, a cooling trend was recorded

If Global Warming Is Real, Why Does It Still Snow?

Some people dismiss climate change and global warming because the earth still experiences cold weather. On cold days, it is common for people to comment out loud or on social media that snow and ice provide direct proof that the earth is not getting any warmer. However, climate scientists have addressed this:

> Even though the planet is getting warmer, cold weather still happens in winter or at very high elevations or high latitudes year-round …
>
> Factors that come into play for regional weather (and indeed global weather) are Earth's seasons, ocean patterns, upper winds, Arctic sea ice, and the shifting shape of the jet stream …
>
> The seasons we experience are a result of Earth's tilted axis as it revolves around the sun. During the North American winter, our hemisphere is tilted away from the sun, leading sunlight to hit us at an angle that makes temperatures lower. While climate change does not affect Earth's tilt, it does have potential implications for many of the other factors that influence winter weather in the U.S. …
>
> Global warming means hotter air, and hotter air can hold more moisture. This translates into heavier precipitation in the form of more intense rain or snow, simply because more moisture is available to storms.[1]

In other words, global warming can actually cause worse snowstorms and harsher winters as well as drier, hotter summers. Weather describes short-term changes; climate tracks long-term changes. Additionally, experts say hurricanes, floods, wildfires, and other natural disasters are becoming worse and more frequent due to climate change caused by global warming.

1. "It's Cold and My Car Is Buried in Snow. Is Global Warming Really Happening?," Union of Concerned Scientists, last updated December 17, 2015. www.ucsusa.org/global_warming/science_and_impacts/science/cold-snow-climate-change.html#.WgX1gWXse-t

between the 1940s and 1970s, when air pollution became a serious problem in developed countries such as the United States. No one was completely sure whether the earth would dip into another ice age or heat up, and some theories stated that global warming could actually cause another ice age by melting the glaciers, causing meltwater to decrease the salinity and temperature of the oceans—exactly what happened during the Younger Dryas period. Most scientists at this time agreed only that the earth's climate was very complicated and that more research was needed before accurate predictions about the effect of human activity on climate change could be made.

In the 1980s, temperatures began to rise again, due to the effects of greenhouse gas emissions and a 1982 volcanic eruption in Mexico. More research followed, including the collection of massive amounts of weather data by oceangoing ships, Earth-orbiting satellites, and consultation among scientists around the globe. As information about the climate increased, a growing number of scientists became more convinced of the existence and potentially serious impacts of global warming, and they began to warn policy makers of the need to address the problem.

AN OUTDATED VIEW

"The Earth was evidently coming out of a relatively cold period in the 1800s so that warming in the past century may be part of this natural recovery."

—John R. Christy, climate and atmospheric science expert at the University of Alabama, in a 1997 testimony

"Testimony of John R. Christy, Committee on Environment and Public Works, Department of Atmospheric Science and Earth System Science Laboratory, University of Alabama in Huntsville, July 10, 1997," U.S. Senate, accessed December 4, 2017, www.epw.senate.gov/105th/chri0710.htm.

Forming a Unified Group

Scientists' efforts to draw attention to climate change were aided in the summer of 1988, when temperatures around the globe soared to the highest levels on record, helping to focus public attention on the issue. That same year, the rising concerns about global warming prompted the world's governments to organize the Intergovernmental Panel on Climate Change (IPCC), an independent group of world climate scientists. Created as part of the UN, the IPCC was asked to examine the available scientific, technical, and socioeconomic evidence on human-created climate change and provide advice to the international community about its impact and possible solutions.

In 1990, the IPCC published its First Assessment Report. The report concluded that increased greenhouse gas emissions caused by human activity "will enhance the greenhouse effect, resulting on average in an additional warming of the Earth's surface."[6]

The 1990 report served as a scientific and technical basis for negotiating a UN agreement on global warming called the UN Framework Convention on Climate Change, adopted in 1992, in which nations pledged to try to stabilize greenhouse gas emissions.

A Second Assessment Report was issued by the IPCC in 1995. At this time, the IPCC again concluded that the increase in global temperatures was likely caused, at least in part, by human activities. However, the report cautioned that it had "not been possible to firmly establish a clear connection between … regional [climate] changes and human activities"[7] because there was not enough data about weather variability over the 20th century. Nevertheless, the IPCC recommended that nations act to reduce emissions, and the report provided information that led to the 1997 adoption of the Kyoto Protocol—an international treaty that set binding targets for the reduction of greenhouse emissions by developed countries.

The IPCC's reports have shown that climate change is real, currently happening, and driven largely by human activity.

In 2001, in its Third Assessment Report, the IPCC announced that the majority of the world's scientists believed the earth was facing significant global warming due to greenhouse gas emissions released by the burning of fossil fuels. The report also said that "there is new and stronger evidence that most of the warming observed over the last 50 years is attributable to human activities."[8] The IPCC predicted that temperatures would most likely rise about 3.8 degrees Fahrenheit (2 degrees Celsius) by 2100 and that this would cause significant climate changes and risks to ecosystems. This assessment helped convince many people that climate change is a serious environmental, social, and political problem. However, the report admitted that there were still some scientific uncertainties about the causes and impacts of global warming that required additional study.

Six years later, in 2007, the IPCC released a Fourth Assessment Report that made its strongest case yet about the dangers of global warming. This time, the IPCC concluded that global warming is "unequivocal," or unmistakable, and that the world's rising temperatures are "very likely"[9] (defined as 90 percent certainty) to be the result of human activities such as the burning of fossil fuels. The report confirmed that the atmospheric levels of carbon dioxide and methane, which are important greenhouse gases, are higher than they have been for 650,000 years. Since the dawn of the industrial era, the report found, concentrations of both gases have increased at a rate unprecedented in more than 10,000 years. The Fifth Assessment Report, released in 2014, repeated these findings with updated figures and an extra warning: Climate change is not something to be dealt with in the future; it is happening right now. The Fifth Assessment Report included a list of the risks associated with climate change, including higher death rates and crop failures, as well as ways societies around the world can change to try to reduce those risks. For example, in a separate document that summarized the IPCC's findings to make them easier for policy makers to understand, the panel identified flooding as one risk North America faces and suggested that governments should make an effort to conserve wetlands—such as the Everglades in Florida—to reduce the intensity of floods. Whether or not policy makers will adopt these suggestions remains to be seen.

FROM STABILITY TO INSTABILITY

"A broad array of scientists ... said the latest [IPCC] analysis was the most sobering view yet of a century of transition—after thousands of years of relatively stable climate conditions—to a new norm of continual change."

—Elisabeth Rosenthal and Andrew C. Revkin, reporters for the *New York Times*

Elisabeth Rosenthal and Andrew C. Revkin, "Panel Issues Bleak Report on Climate Change," *New York Times*, February 2, 2007. www.nytimes.com/2007/02/02/science/earth/02cnd-climate.html.

Most Scientists Agree

According to most commentators and scientists, the IPCC reports establish that there is a scientific consensus that climate change is occurring and that it is the result of human activities. In 2004, Naomi Oreskes, a science professor at the University of California, San Diego, surveyed 928 abstracts of peer-reviewed papers related to global climate change and found that none of them disagreed with the IPCC position. In a widely discussed article published in the journal *Science*, Oreskes stated, "Scientists publishing in the peer-reviewed literature agree with IPCC, the National Academy of Sciences, and the public statements of their professional societies [that global warming is caused by human activities]."[10] Peer-reviewed literature has been checked for quality by other researchers, so it is more reliable.

Today, most scientists continue to support the conclusions of the IPCC. In a joint statement issued after the IPCC's Fourth Assessment Report was released, science academies in the major industrialized countries—including Canada, France, Germany, Italy, Japan, Russia, the United Kingdom, and the United States—as well as a number of developing nations, stated, "It is unequivocal that the climate is changing, and it is very likely that this is predominantly caused by the increasing human interference with the atmosphere. These changes will transform the environmental conditions on Earth unless counter-measures are taken."[11]

Natural Instability

Experts agree that the earth's climate is naturally unstable and that the Holocene Period's relative stability is unusual, which is why many scientists originally rejected the idea that humans were causing global warming and climate change. Author Bill Bryson explained,

> Thanks to ice cores from Greenland we have a detailed record of climate for something over a hundred thousand years, and what is found there is not comforting. It shows that for most of its recent history Earth has been nothing like the stable and tranquil place that civilization has known, but rather has lurched violently between periods of warmth and brutal chill ...
>
> There is no reason to suppose that this stretch of climatic stability should last much longer ... It is natural to suppose that global warming would act as a useful counterweight to the Earth's tendency to plunge back into glacial conditions. However, as [journalist Elizabeth] Kolbert has pointed out, when you are confronted with a fluctuating and unpredictable climate "the last thing you'd want to do is conduct a vast unsupervised experiment on it."[1]

Recent research has proven that humans do indeed have a large effect on global warming, which is ruining the stability of the Holocene Period. Although the climate would likely have changed on its own eventually, human involvement has made that change come much more quickly.

1. Bill Bryson, *A Short History of Nearly Everything*. New York, NY: Broadway Books, 2003. "Ice Time."

Climate Change Denial

Despite the agreement of scientific opinion on the causes and dangers of global warming, many skeptics, or disbeliev- ers, remain. Most skeptics agree that global temperatures are

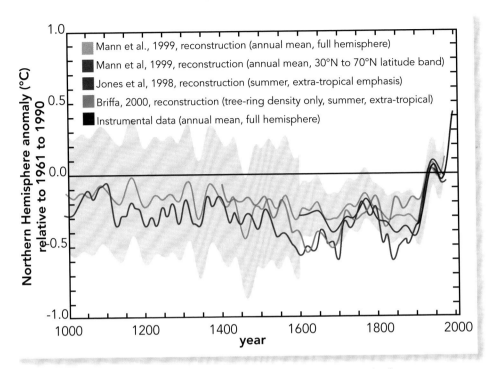

The hockey stick shape made by Mann's research—and the research of scientists who found similar results—can be seen here.

increasing, but they believe temperature fluctuations are relatively small and primarily caused by natural forces. A Gallup poll in March 2017 showed that only 50 percent of Americans believe in and are concerned about climate change. The remaining 50 percent were divided into two groups, which Gallup called "Mixed Middle" and "Cool Skeptics." Those who belonged to the Mixed Middle group—31 percent of poll respondents—were unsure whether climate change is really happening, whether it is happening because of humans, and whether it is a serious threat. Cool Skeptics, which accounted for 19 percent of respondents, were firmly convinced that climate change news is made up, that global warming is not affected by human activity, and that the whole thing is nothing to worry about.

One area of disagreement, for example, revolves around a temperature graph used by global warming advocates. This has been called the "hockey stick graph" because it is slightly shaped like a hockey stick placed on its side: "After a long period of relatively minor temperature variations (the 'shaft'), it showed a sharp mercury upswing during the last century or so (the 'blade')."[12]. This graph, published by geoscientist Michael Mann and 2 colleagues, shows that there have been no large global temperature variations over the past 1,000 years in the Northern Hemisphere, except during the last 100 years, when temperatures have sharply peaked, presumably due to humans' use of fossil fuels. Some critics of this graph say Mann made mistakes in his research or deliberately used research results he knew were wrong, although an investigation into these claims has proven them false. Others accuse the graph of conveniently ignoring natural temperature fluctuations such as the Medieval Warm Period and the Little Ice Age. Since the Medieval Warm Period produced temperatures much warmer than those the earth is experiencing today, critics have argued, the earth today may simply be experiencing a similar natural warming cycle following the end of the Little Ice Age. However, recent research has found that the Medieval Warm Period was not as warm as people previously thought; William D'Andrea of Columbia University's Lamont-Doherty Earth Observatory reported in 2012 that "summer temperatures in the Svalbard Archipelago, a group of islands in the Arctic Ocean about 400 miles north of Norway, have been between 3.6°F and 4.5°F higher over the past 25 years, on average, than the summers the Vikings enjoyed."[13] Since Mann's graph was published in 1998, multiple other studies have found the same results.

A MOCKING STATEMENT

"Global warming isn't real because I was cold today! Also great news: World hunger is over because I just ate."

–Stephen Colbert, comedian

Stephen Colbert (@StephenAtHome), Twitter, November 18, 2014, 8:40 p.m. twitter.com/stephenathome/status/534929076726009856?lang=en

Skeptics also note that while parts of the planet are warming, such as much of the Northern Hemisphere and the Arctic, the Southern Hemisphere and Antarctica are not experiencing any statistically significant warming. In fact, researchers agree that although the Antarctic Peninsula—a sliver of land that projects into the ocean toward the southern tip of South America—is seeing a rapid rise in temperatures that is causing the melting of glacier ice, most of Antarctica has not registered any warming trend since researchers began studying it in the late 1970s. In 2014, NASA, which has taken photos of the earth from space for decades to help scientists study trends, reported that the amount of ice in the water near Antarctica had reached a new record maximum, which many climate change deniers claimed disproved global warming. However, NASA explained,

> The new Antarctic sea ice record reflects the diversity and complexity of Earth's environments … Just as the temperatures in some regions of the planet are colder than average, even in our warming world, Antarctic sea ice has been increasing and bucking the overall trend of ice loss.

> "The planet as a whole is doing what was expected in terms of warming. Sea ice as a whole is decreasing as expected, but just like with global warming, not every location with sea ice will have a downward trend in ice extent," [senior NASA scientist Claire] Parkinson said.[14]

Some climate change deniers use the amount of ice on Antarctica, shown here, to back up their argument that global warming is not real.

Other criticisms of global warming science continue to create a seed of doubt among the public and policy makers about whether climate change is truly a threat. These include claims that directly contradict the available scientific evidence—for instance, that glaciers are growing rather than melting, that greenhouse gases have no effect on the climate, that the oceans are getting cooler rather than warmer, and that the planet has been warmer in the past than it is now with no ill effects on plant or animal life. Many people also misunderstand how global warming affects climate change, assuming that if global warming were really getting worse, there would be no ice left on the planet. These arguments come from a misunderstanding of how complex the earth's climate is and how complicated some of the effects of climate change can be.

Politics and the economy also play a large part in climate change denial. Donald Trump has often stated that he believes global warming is a hoax. In 2012, he posted on Twitter, "The concept of global warming was created by and for the Chinese in order to make U.S. manufacturing non-competitive."[15] He repeated this idea during the 2016 presidential debates. No proof has been found to back up this statement; in fact, some evidence has been found that disproves this claim, such as the Chinese president pledging to fight climate change and China's approval of the Paris climate agreement. However, many of Trump's supporters believed what he said and thought he was exposing something that had been kept secret for a long time.

While Trump's statements about China remain unproven, it is true that business is an important part of the climate change debate. For this reason, as a team of journalists reported in 2016, large oil companies such as ExxonMobil deliberately kept their knowledge of how global warming affects climate change a secret. According to National Public Radio (NPR), ExxonMobil's executives and scientists knew by the late 1970s—possibly even earlier—that burning fossil fuels had a negative effect on the planet. NPR quoted an Exxon memo from 1979:

Models predict that the present trend of fossil fuel use will lead to dramatic climatic changes within the next 75 years ... Should it be deemed necessary to maintain atmospheric CO2 levels to prevent significant climatic changes, dramatic changes in patterns of energy use would be required.[16]

Since these findings would have hurt their profits, Exxon lied to the public, telling people that oil had nothing to do with climate change and encouraging people to keep buying their products. This is similar to tactics used by tobacco and pharmaceutical companies, which told people that cigarettes and opioid painkillers were neither harmful nor addictive—lies that ultimately led to many deaths.

Because of a combination of misinformation from oil companies and promises from Trump to revive the energy industry, many people believe that cutting down on the use of coal and oil will hurt the economy and put many people out of work. This problem is a complex one. In some places, such as West Virginia and eastern Kentucky, entire towns have been sustained by the coal industry, and as fewer people use coal, these towns have encountered severe financial troubles. Many people have blamed renewable resources for this, which makes them suspicious of climate change claims and more willing to believe sources that say climate change is not real or not serious; if a family's income relies on coal or oil, they will be more concerned with how they are going to put food on the table now than the impact on the

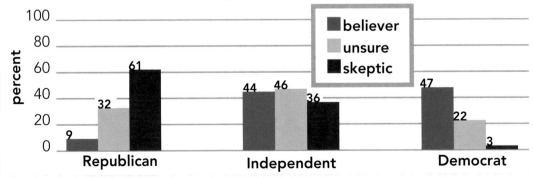

Belief in Climate Change Based on Political Affiliation

As this information from a 2017 Gallup poll shows, a person's political beliefs and climate change beliefs often seem to be connected.

Information Avoidance

Humans have a tendency to believe what they want to believe because it makes them happier or more comfortable—a phenomenon psychologists call information avoidance. Sometimes this means ignoring certain information, while other times it means seeking out the information that makes people happiest; for instance, by looking for articles that seem to prove climate change is not real. Carnegie Mellon University explained why this is a problem:

> Questionable evidence is often treated as credible when it confirms what someone wants to believe—as is the case of discredited research linking vaccines to autism. And evidence that meets the rigorous demands of science is often discounted if it goes against what people want to believe, as illustrated by widespread dismissal of climate change.
>
> Information avoidance can be harmful, for example, when people miss opportunities to treat serious diseases early on or fail to learn about better financial investments that could prepare them for retirement. It also has large societal implications.[1]

The researchers explained that giving people information that contradicts their belief often does not work because in some cases, people will simply ignore it, and in other cases, being proven wrong will actually strengthen a person's belief that they are correct, especially if the information is presented aggressively. They suggested that it is better for people to "find ways not only to expose people to conflicting information, but to increase people's receptivity to information that challenges what they believe and want to believe."[2]

1 Shilo Rea, "Information Avoidance: How People Select Their Own Reality," Carnegie Mellon University, March 13, 2017. www.cmu.edu/news/stories/archives/2017/march/information-avoidance.html

2 Quoted in Rhea, "Information Avoidance."

environment years from now. In truth, however, natural gas and rising coal prices are more to blame for the decrease in coal consumption, and switching to renewable energy across the United States would open up thousands of new jobs, many of which would be less dangerous than coal mining.

Another reason why people deny climate change is because facing it is uncomfortable. If people acknowledge that climate change is a real, serious problem, they will have to change their lifestyles, and many people are unwilling to do so. *Quartz* reported that some of the top climate change Google searches in 2017 included "why climate change is not important," "why climate change is not man made," "why climate change is good," and "why climate change is fake." Finding websites that support these mindsets makes some people feel more comfortable and secure. They do not have to feel afraid for the future of humanity or the environment, and they do not have to make any changes to their routine, such as walking places instead of driving. However, ignoring the problem will only continue to make it worse, which means people will eventually have to make changes anyway. These may include small changes, such as being unable to afford coffee because climate change has wiped out most of the coffee bean crops in Mexico, or large changes, such as being forced to move to another state or country because a family can no longer live comfortably where they are. Facing the climate change crisis head-on is the only way to prevent it from getting worse.

CHAPTER 2

The Uncertainty of the Future

Although the majority of climate scientists now agree that global warming is a real, dangerous issue caused by human activity, many uncertainties remain. One is how quickly the world is heating up; scientists are revising their estimates all the time as new research shows that global warming is speeding up. Another is whether the trend can be reversed. Scientists have been warning for years that actions need to be put into place immediately—in fact, these actions should have been put into place years ago—to stop global warming. Many policy makers have ignored these warnings; some have made no changes at all, while others have made decisions that benefit companies but do further harm to the environment.

SOME THINGS ARE CERTAIN

"Despite all the complexities, a firm and ever-growing body of evidence points to a clear picture: the world is warming, this warming is due to human activity increasing levels of green-house gases in the atmosphere, and if emissions continue unabated the warming will too, with increasingly serious consequences."

–Michael Le Page, writer and editor for *New Scientist*

Michael Le Page, "Climate Change: A Guide for the Perplexed," *New Scientist*, May 16, 2007. www.newscientist.com/article/dn11462-climate-change-a-guide-for-the-perplexed/

Other uncertainties involve which specific changes will happen—a fact skeptics often use to try to deny climate change, claiming that if researchers cannot say exactly what will happen, it is likely nothing will happen. Again, this type of argument comes from a misunderstanding of how difficult it is to predict how the earth will behave. Climate scientists research possible effects of global warming and give several different outcomes that are likely to happen, but they are unable to say with complete certainty because there are so many different variables.

A Faster Rate of Change

Temperatures vary naturally from year to year, but most climate scientists agree that average global temperatures have risen about 1.3 degrees Fahrenheit (0.7 degree Celsius) during the last century, with two-thirds of this warming occurring since the 1970s. If this trend continues, experts believe the temperature will rise 2 to 6 degrees Fahrenheit (1.1 to 3.3 degrees Celsius) within the next century. Temperature measurements available since 1860 indicate that the 2010s have been the warmest decade since that time.

Some skeptics point out that 1934 was the hottest year on record in the United States, claiming that this shows the earth is actually getting cooler, not warmer. Other critics have suggested that worldwide temperatures during the 1990s may have recorded hotter than past decades because hundreds of measuring stations were shut down in cold regions of the world, such as the Soviet Union. Also, critics say, many once-rural measuring stations may have been surrounded by urban sprawl—suburban developments with numerous roads and concrete parking lots that are known to absorb more sunlight and become much hotter than the countryside.

However, even taking these explanations into account, it is clear to most researchers that the earth has warmed, particularly in recent decades. Climate change science takes into account global temperature changes, and the United States is only 2 percent of the earth's surface. Additionally, temperatures have warmed more in the ocean than on land, so the urban sprawl argument does not carry much weight. As has previously been discussed, global warming and climate change do not affect all parts of the globe exactly the same way. Looking at average global temperatures shows that overall, the earth is getting warmer. To the average person, the amount of warming so far may seem quite small, but scientists say even minor temperature changes can have significant effects on the climate and ecosystems.

Some climate skeptics say there is no problem because the earth has naturally warmed in the past, but NASA explained why researchers are worried:

> When global warming has happened at various times in the past two million years, it has taken the planet about 5,000 years to warm 5 degrees. The predicted rate of warming for the next century is at least 20 times faster. This rate of change is extremely unusual.[17]

The Problem of Tropical Expansion

According to researchers at the National Oceanic and Atmospheric Administration (NOAA), a U.S. government science agency, the tropics are rapidly expanding due to global warming. In an article published in 2007 in the magazine *Nature Geoscience*, the NOAA researchers found that the tropical zone—a geographic band around the earth's equator—was spreading both northward and southward toward the poles. In addition, the study found that this expansion was happening at a rate much faster than predicted by climate models. Under the most extreme scenario predicted by climate models, the tropical zone was supposed to expand by about 2 degrees latitude (about 120 miles, or 200 kilometers) by the end of the 21st century, but NOAA found this worst-case scenario has already happened. The tropical zone includes Florida and parts of the U.S. Southwest, as well as southern Australia, southern Africa, and parts of the European Mediterranean region. As of early 2018, this expansion is still happening, which is leading to worse droughts and less overall rainfall in the tropics.

A Difficult Trend to Reverse

Because greenhouse gases already released into the atmosphere will linger for many years and because the earth is slow to adjust to these changes, the climate is expected to continue to warm in the future. In fact, this continued warming will occur even if governments act today to reduce emissions from cars, power plants, and other sources. Climatologists call this "committed warming." It would be impossible to suddenly stop emitting all carbon dioxide, but even if that were to somehow happen in one day, experts say it would take about 40 years for the climate to stabilize, and even then, the earth would remain warmer than it had been in the past.

In its 2007 report, the IPCC said the degree of global warming will vary depending on the level of future greenhouse emissions. It developed six emission scenarios and, using sophisticated climate simulation programs, projected "best estimate" and "likely range" future temperatures for each scenario. Overall, the IPCC projected a range of temperature increases between 2 and 11.5 degrees Fahrenheit (1.1 to 6.4 degrees Celsius) by the end of the century.

The most optimistic IPCC scenario, for example, assumed that emissions could be dramatically lowered as a result of a rapid change toward a service and information economy and a quick shift toward clean energy technologies. Under these conditions, the IPCC predicted a likely range of 0.5 to 1.6 degrees Fahrenheit (0.3 to 0.9 degree Celsius) and a best estimate temperature rise of about 1.1 degrees Fahrenheit (0.62 degree Celsius) by 2100. In its 2014 report, the IPCC repeated this advice, stating that emissions must be cut immediately, renewable energy and products must be used by 2050, and fossil fuels should no longer be used by 2100.

However, in many countries, especially the United States, little to no change has occurred. In this case, the IPCC concluded in 2007 that there may be twice as much warming over the next two decades as in the past, and the worst-case scenario predicted by the IPCC suggested that the world might see drastically higher temperatures over the next century. This scenario assumes that there will be rapid economic growth and continued reliance on fossil-intensive energy production and consumption, and thus continuing high levels of greenhouse emissions, and this is what has occurred in most countries in the past decade. If this continues, the IPCC says the world would likely see temperatures soaring somewhere in the range of 4.3 to 11.5 degrees Fahrenheit (2.4 to 6.4 degrees Celsius), with a best estimate that temperatures would increase by 7.2 degrees Fahrenheit (4 degrees Celsius) by 2100.

Hurricane Irma, shown here, was one of the worst storms on record. Researchers say this is likely because of climate change.

The 2014 report stated that many effects of global warming can already be observed in the climate, and these issues often cause a chain reaction of problems. For instance, the ocean has become 26 percent more acidic since the Industrial Revolution due to its absorption of carbon dioxide, which has had a negative effect on marine life. This affects the amount of seafood available for animals and humans to eat. The ocean has also become much warmer, which, experts say, is why the 2017 hurricane season was so much worse than usual. Warmer water creates more energy for storms that form over the ocean, which means harder rain, higher winds, and more flooding when they hit land—all of which contribute to more death and destruction. *Scientific American* magazine explained,

> *The dynamic between storms and warming oceans occurs in part because of the role hurricanes play in our climate system: they*

rebalance Earth's heat. The storms remove heat from tropical oceans in the form of moisture and pump the heat up into the atmosphere, where heat is redistributed and radiated out into space.[18]

This means that as the oceans get warmer, hurricanes will become more frequent and more intense. This has already been seen with hurricanes Harvey and Irma, both of which hit land in August 2017. According to CNN, Hurricane Irma was "the strongest Atlantic basin hurricane ever recorded outside the Gulf of Mexico and the Caribbean Sea."[19] It lasted 12 days, covered 650 miles (1,046 km), and affected 9 U.S. states as well as some Caribbean islands. Scientists say that if no action is taken to reduce emissions, this trend will keep growing worse.

A WORSENING SITUATION

"Heat waves will occur more often and last longer ... extreme precipitation events will become more intense and frequent in many regions. The oceans will continue to warm and acidify, and global mean [average] sea level to rise."

–IPCC's Fifth Assessment Report

Quoted in John Light, "The 10 Things You Need to Know from the New IPCC Climate Report," *Grist*, November 2, 2014. grist.org/climate-energy/the-10-things-you-need-to-know-from-the-new-ipcc-climate-report/

The Feedback Effect

The earth's climate is highly complex, and experts say it is possible that the climate could change even more rapidly than scientists have predicted. For instance, recent research has shown that the ocean is heating up 13 percent faster than experts previously thought, and this rate is only increasing. One factor that cannot be figured into the climate models used by IPCC scientists is known as climate feedbacks—changes in climate that occur in response to rising temperatures. These feedbacks can either increase the effects of global warming (positive feedback) or decrease it (negative feedback). These terms can be confusing because it seems like positive feedback would mean something that makes the climate situation better, but in fact, it is something that makes it worse. It may help to think of positive and negative in terms of adding or subtracting heat—although the situation is generally a little more complex than that.

Melting sea ice and glaciers could make global warming worse in more ways than one.

One example of positive feedback that could produce additional warming involves melting Arctic sea ice. This melting could, in turn, add to the earth's warming because the loss of large sections of highly reflective ice would mean that less sunlight is reflected back into space and more of this energy is absorbed by the oceans. Similarly, if higher temperatures produce more drought and more forest fires, the decrease in greenery that absorbs carbon dioxide and the burning of these organic matters is expected to add carbon dioxide to the atmosphere and increase global warming. Some scientists are also concerned that as the amount of carbon dioxide in the air increases, plants' ability to absorb it will decrease, making it accumulate more quickly in the atmosphere.

Another positive feedback that could have a significant effect on temperatures is water vapor. A warmer atmosphere creates more water vapor in the atmosphere, which holds more greenhouse gases. Experts know this will contribute to faster global warming but are unsure of exactly how many degrees it will add to an already warm Earth.

These positive feedbacks, however, could potentially be offset by negative feedbacks. An example of a possible negative feedback is the creation of more low clouds from the increased evaporation that will be caused by warmer surface temperatures. A greater number of low, thick clouds would tend to cool the climate by reflecting more sunlight back into space before it reaches the ground, reducing the amount of energy that is absorbed by the earth's landmasses and oceans. Another negative feedback would be the growth of new plants in areas with increased rainfall or a warmer climate. More plants means more absorption of carbon dioxide, which would slow global warming.

IGNORING THE WARNINGS

"The good news is our understanding of the climate system and our impact on it has improved immensely. The bad news is that the more we know, the more precarious [uncertain] the future looks ... If the last IPCC report was a wake up call, this [2007] one is a screaming siren."

—Stephanie Tunmore, climate and energy campaigner for Greenpeace International

Quoted in "Key Players React to the IPCC Global Warming Report." *Christian Science Monitor,* February 8, 2007. www.csmonitor.com/2007/0208/p25s01-sten.html.

There is a lot of uncertainty surrounding feedback effects because although researchers are fairly certain of how the earth will change if they occur, they cannot say for certain which of these changes will happen. As *Forbes* noted in an article about the uncertainties of climate change, "There's considerable uncertainty as to the feedback effects on ocean circulation. For example, it's 100% certain that a shutdown of the Atlantic Meridional Overturning Circulation would have terrible consequences for the planet, but it's very hard to predict when or if that might happen."[20]

STAYING HOPEFUL

"The situation is by no means hopeless. Major advances and technological breakthroughs are being made in the United States and throughout the world that are giving us the tools to cut carbon emissions dramatically, break our dependency on fossil fuels and move to energy efficiency and sustainable energy ... With strong governmental leadership the crisis of global warming is not only solvable; it can be done while improving the standard of living of the people of this country and others around the world."

—Bernie Sanders, Vermont senator and former presidential candidate

Bernie Sanders, "Global Warming Is Reversible," *Nation*, November 27, 2007. www.thenation.com/article/global-warming-reversible/.

The Methane Problem

Although carbon dioxide is the greenhouse gas that is discussed most often, another gas called methane is also causing problems. It does not stay in the atmosphere as long as carbon dioxide, but while it is there, it causes global warming much faster than carbon dioxide. According to Dr. Bob Talbot, the director of the Institute for Climate and Atmospheric Science, "Methane has a global warming potential of 28 over a 100-year time frame, a measure developed to reflect how much heat it traps in the atmosphere, meaning a ton of methane will absorb 28 times as much thermal energy as a ton of carbon dioxide."[21] After 10 to 20 years, methane decays and turns into carbon dioxide.

Methane can come from man-made sources such as oil and gas production as well as natural sources such as wetlands, glaciers, and animal digestion. For instance, when cows burp or pass gas, they are releasing methane. Scientists previously thought methane emissions from cows were not a large problem, but recent research has shown that they produce 11 percent more methane than past studies indicated. As the world's population grows and people's consumption of beef and dairy increase, forests are cut down to create grazing room for more

The Doomsday Vault Scare

In February 2007, a facility known as the Svalbard Global Seed Vault—sometimes nicknamed the Doomsday Vault—was opened on Norway's Svalbard archipelago. This facility is able to hold a stockpile of 2.25 billion seeds, and experts are attempting to gather seed samples from as many different kinds of plants as possible. These are stored in the vault, which is kept cold by permafrost (frozen soil) and thick rock, freezing the seeds to keep them fresh. This way, if a type of food is wiped out by disease, climate change, or any other event, the world will have a backup. There are other seed banks in the world, and the Svalbard vault stores backup samples of seeds in case something happens to the other seed banks; *Popular Science* magazine called it "a backup for the backups."[1]

In October 2016, due to unusually warm weather and rainfall levels, it was reported on social media that the Svalbard vault had flooded and the seeds were lost. Fortunately, this turned out to be the result of people panicking and spreading news before they had fully confirmed the details. A spokesperson for the vault said that while it was true water leaked into the tunnel that led to the vault, the seed bank did not flood and the seeds were unharmed. However, as *Popular Science* noted, "This is Svalbard: land of snow, ice, and polar bears. Meltwater is still worrying, even if it isn't an immediate panic-inducing threat."[2] To prevent future accidents, the Norwegian government is taking steps to make the building even more waterproof.

Although the seeds in the Svalbard Global Seed Vault were not damaged by meltwater, the fact that there was meltwater entering the vault at all is a problem.

1. Mary Beth Griggs, "Turns Out the Svalbard Seed Vault Is Probably Fine," *Popular Science*, May 22, 2017, www.popsci.com/seed-vault-flooding.
2. Griggs, "Turns Out the Svalbard Seed Vault Is Probably Fine."

cows. This has a serious effect on global warming: At the same time, carbon-absorbing forests are disappearing and the number of methane-producing cows is increasing.

Farmers have cut down trees to make room for more cows, which has made global warming worse in two ways at once.

Another source of methane could be the world's oceans and glaciers. According to Tessa Hill, a professor in the department of Earth and Planetary Sciences at the University of California, Davis, as oceans warm, oil and gases seep out of the ocean floor, including methane. Glaciers, too, release a form of methane as they begin to melt, adding to the earth's greenhouse effect. As Hill explained, "These petroleum seeps appear to be activated by periods of climate change ... If the Earth is already in a mode of warming, they 'turn on' and become more active, which promotes further warming."[22]

Tipping Points

The uncertainty of climate change means some predictions never come true. For instance, some researchers have proposed that the effects of global warming could trigger a major climate change that could suddenly plunge the world back into another ice age rather than the warming period predicted by the IPCC. At the center of this theory is the Gulf Stream—a strong ocean current that transports warm water from the tropics to northwestern Europe, giving it a temperate climate similar to that of the United States even though it is located at a much higher latitude, more like the location of Alaska. The Gulf Stream is driven mostly by differences in water temperature and salinity: Warmer waters from the tropics evaporate and are cooled as they head north, and these salty, cool waters then settle to the bottom of the sea, where they form a massive undersea river that flows south down to the Southern, or Antarctic, Ocean. The process then repeats, creating what has been referred to as a conveyor belt in the ocean that helps regulate temperatures between the Northern and Southern Hemispheres.

According to researchers, however, melting polar ice caps and the melting glaciers in Greenland caused by global warming could add huge amounts of fresh water to the northern Atlantic Ocean, and this fresh water could disrupt the Gulf Stream conveyor process because it will not sink like salty water. Such a slowing or shutting down of the Gulf Stream, some scientists speculated, could cause a rapid cooling of temperatures within a few decades, possibly causing a little ice age like the one that occurred a few centuries ago and contributing to harsher winters, droughts, and crop failures in some countries. The worst-case scenario was that the world could return to a full-blown ice age, a prospect that could challenge the ability of humans to survive around the globe.

Until recently, scientists were unsure whether the world would get too hot or too cold.

Scientists once believed that such a major climate shift could only occur gradually over hundreds of years. However, newly developed drilling equipment has allowed scientists in recent years to extract and examine ice cores from some of Greenland's most ancient glaciers. Thanks to this new technology, scientists were able to look at individual years of snow. What they learned is that the earth has often transitioned from ice-age weather to temperate weather like that of today in a matter of just two to three years. The shocking news is that instead of a slow change in climate, the earth is capable of making a major climate shift when it reaches a certain tipping point. Once this tipping point is passed, the damage cannot be reversed, and scientists fear certain parts of the world are close to that point. For instance, if the West Antarctic ice sheet collapses, there is no way it can be built back up, and the effects of less ice and more meltwater will have significant impacts on the climate.

Although the earth goes through natural periods of cold and warmth—with a glacial period lasting 90,000 years and a warm period lasting 10,000—researchers now say temperatures have risen enough in recent years to delay the next ice age by another 100,000 years. Some people believe this is a good thing because an ice age would have as much of an impact on human, plant, and animal life as a much hotter world would. Climate change skeptics say this means global warming is actually good for humanity.

However, while a little bit of extra carbon dioxide in the air years ago may have been helpful in avoiding sheets of glaciers, humans have released too much of the gas too quickly, causing other serious problems that must be dealt with—and the level of carbon dioxide is rising all the time. Earth's climate is in a delicate balance, and just because a glacial period was avoided does not mean there will be no other negative consequences. In September 2016, *Motherboard* magazine reported researchers' findings from the Mauna Loa Observatory in Hawai'i: The amount of carbon dioxide in the atmosphere has reached 400 ppm—the highest amount since observation began at that spot in 1958—and scientists believe it is stuck there for the foreseeable future.

CHAPTER 3

The Dangers of Climate Change

Many climate changes have already begun happening as a result of global warming, and some of these changes have sparked other changes that do not seem directly related to the climate. Because the whole planet needs to maintain a specific, delicate balance, even small changes can have a big impact, and since everything in the environment is connected, changes in one area generally causes changes in another. The effects of climate change reach far beyond warmer weather.

Visible Changes

Rising global temperatures have already had a major impact on the environment and ecosystems in many regions of the world. The 2007 IPCC report, for example, found that numerous environmental changes can be clearly linked to climate change. Arctic glaciers are rapidly melting, creating more and larger glacial lakes and increased, earlier spring runoff into snow-fed rivers. Mountainous regions are experiencing more rock avalanches, and warmer temperatures are causing permafrost to thaw, causing increasing ground instability in northern latitudes.

The IPCC has also said warming water temperatures are causing changes in some Arctic and Antarctic ecosystems. Changes in ice cover, water salinity and acidity, oxygen levels, and water circulation, for example, are harming algae, fish, and plankton (microscopic marine life that provide food for many larger marine creatures). Rising sea levels are also causing losses of coastal wetlands and mangrove forests, which in turn contribute to more coastal flooding. Other changes are occurring in land-based biological systems. Events such as the unfolding of leaves, laying of eggs, and migration, which generally happen in the spring, are now happening earlier, and many plants and animals are moving northward and to higher altitudes as temperatures warm. Many experts believe that larger Arctic creatures, such as polar bears and the seals they feed on, are starving and well on their way to extinction.

Changes in the ocean threaten marine life, which means less food for both animals and humans.

Reporter Timothy Egan provided examples of climate changes that have already happened in Alaska:

In Shishmaref [Alaska], on the Chukchi Sea just south of the Arctic Circle, it means high water eating away so many houses and buildings that people … [may] move the entire village inland.

In Barrow, the northernmost city in North America, it means coping with mosquitoes in a place where they once were nonexistent, and rescuing hunters trapped on breakaway ice at a time of year when such things once were unheard of.

From Fairbanks to the north, where wildfires have been burning … it means living with hydraulic jacks to keep houses from slouching on foundations that used to be frozen all year. Permafrost, they say, no longer is permanent …

*On the Kenai Peninsula, a recreation wonderland a few hours'
drive from Anchorage, it means living in a 4 million-acre spruce
forest that has been killed by beetles, the largest loss of trees to
insects ever recorded in North America, federal officials say. Government scientists tied the event to rising temperatures, which allow the beetles to reproduce at twice their normal rate.*[23]

Effects on Humans

Human health, too, is already being affected by climate change.
In Europe, heat waves have led to a rise in heat-related deaths in
recent years. Extreme temperatures in the summer of 2003, for
example, are believed to have caused 35,000 deaths in European
Union countries. In fact, climate researchers say that since 1880,
extremely hot days have become almost three times more frequent in the region, and the length of these heat waves has
doubled. The American Southwest has also experienced scorch-
ing heat waves. Other parts of the world are noticing different
health threats as a result of rising temperatures. In 2007, countries in Southeast Asia, such as Vietnam, Indonesia, Thailand,
and Cambodia, experienced one of the worst-ever outbreaks of
dengue fever, a serious illness carried by mosquitoes that causes
fever, joint pain, and sometimes death. Dr. Thawat Suntrajarn,
director of Bangkok Chain Hospital, explained, "Experts say
it's partly due to global warming because it's increased the
amount of water, not only sea water, but fresh water where
mosquitoes breed."[24] This is also the result of floods caused by
hurricanes, which create large areas of standing water where
disease-carrying insects can breed.

In the western United States, wildfires made worse by prolonged periods of drought have caused health issues as well due
to the increased amount of smoke and ash in the air. All over
the world, pollen levels are rising, making people with allergies
sicker than in the past. Also, carbon dioxide, which is a cause of
global warming rather than an effect, is having negative effects
on health by making air pollution worse. When people breathe
in polluted air, they develop problems such as asthma, bronchi-
tis, heart disease, and possibly some types of cancer.

Moreover, periods of severe weather—both heavy precipitation and sustained droughts—have become more common, and this has caused a decline in food production in some parts of the world. One of the areas most affected is the continent of Africa, which in recent years has been experiencing both torrential floods and severe drought—each a threat to the region's food supply. In 2002 and 2003, for example, southern Africa suffered from a drought that caused a serious food deficit in which an estimated 14.4 million people needed food assistance, and in 2007, West Africa was hit with heavy rains and widespread flooding that also destroyed crops. In 2007, Australia, too, faced an unprecedented drought that led to severe water restrictions, crop failures, and a drying up of rivers in the Murray-Darling river system—the source of irrigation for much of the country's food production. In the United States, water shortages that have long plagued the western states have now begun to affect the East. In the fall of 2007, for example, southeastern states such as Florida, Georgia, and Alabama experienced a drought of historic proportions. The shortages of food and water caused by droughts and flooding have severe health effects on the affected populations, including malnutrition and malnourishment.

Drought and floods both threaten global food supplies.

The IPCC also expects climate change to contribute to increased rates of illness, injuries, and death for people around the globe. Developing countries, many of which are already struggling to cope with extreme poverty and epidemics, will likely see a rise in malnutrition, diarrhea, and stunted child growth and development due to decreased food production. Children, the elderly, and the poor are the most at risk, and some may not be able to survive. A study by scientists from the World Health Organization (WHO) in 2002 found that 154,000 people already die every year from these effects of climate change, and it said these numbers could double by 2020.

PUT THE ENVIRONMENT FIRST

"When the last tree is cut, the last fish is caught, and the last river is polluted; when to breathe the air is sickening, you will realize, too late, that wealth is not in bank accounts and that you can't eat money."

—Alanis Obomsawin, documentary filmmaker

Quoted in "When the Last Tree Is Cut Down, the Last Fish Eaten, and the Last Stream Poisoned, You Will Realize That You Cannot Eat Money," Quote Investigator, October 20, 2011. quoteinvestigator. com/2011/10/20/last-tree-cut/.

Since tropical weather is expected to expand as temperatures rise, another health effect is that dangerous tropical diseases could spread into higher altitudes and latitudes. Malaria, for example, is a disease transmitted by mosquitoes, which thrive in warmer temperatures. As temperatures rise, many experts expect mosquitoes to travel farther and expand the territory subject to malaria infections. A similar threat may come from Lyme disease, which is carried by deer ticks. In addition, experts say the indirect effects of global warming, such as drought and flooding, could send millions of rural residents fleeing into the cities, where dense housing conditions could lead to the spread of many other highly infectious illnesses such as tuberculosis, human immunodeficiency virus (HIV), and acquired immunodeficiency syndrome (AIDS). Overcrowding would likely result in food and housing shortages as well.

Scientists, however, cannot predict exactly how diseases will respond to the multitude of anticipated climate changes. As Stephen Morse of Columbia University said, "Environmental changes have always been associated with the appearance of new diseases or the arrival of old diseases in new places. With more [global warming] changes, we can expect more surprises."[25]

Effects on the Weather

As temperatures increase, experts say these trends will get worse. Over the next century, the IPCC predicts more extreme weather and more ice melts, accompanied by potentially devastating rises in sea levels. Weather changes will also include more severe heat waves, more periods of drought and fires, and more frequent and intense storms, hurricanes, and tornadoes.

However, not all regions will be affected in the same way. The 2007 IPCC report, for example, said, "Changes in precipitation and temperature lead to changes in runoff and water availability. Runoff is projected with high confidence to increase by 10 to 40% by mid-century at higher latitudes and in some wet tropical areas ... and decrease by 10 to 30% over some dry regions at mid-latitudes and dry tropics."[26] This means dry regions of the world will get drier and see more frequent and larger fires, and wet regions will see more and bigger storms and increased risks from flooding or blizzards.

If sea levels rise too high, parts of the world's coast will become uninhabitable. Shown here is an Indonesian cemetery that was flooded by rising sea levels.

In addition, melting glaciers, sea ice, and snow, together with ocean expansion resulting from increased water temperatures, are expected to cause sea levels to rise dramatically. The IPCC climate models project that by the end of this century, the global average sea level will rise between 7 and 23 inches (18 and 58 cm) above the 1980 to 1999 average. Even bigger changes are possible, however, if Arctic and Antarctic ice sheets melt faster than expected. According to Bryson, "If all the ice sheets melted, sea levels would rise by two hundred feet—the height of a twenty-story building—and every coastal city in the world would be inundated [flooded]."[27] This is a worst-case scenario that will not happen immediately and may never happen at all, but even a relatively small sea-level rise could threaten coasts, cities, and low-lying islands around the world and cause flooding that could kill millions. As *National Geographic* explained in 2001,

> *Over a third of the world's population now lives within 62 miles (100 kilometers) of a shoreline, and 13 of the world's 20 largest cities are located on a coast. Unfortunately, the world's booming coastal population faces an uphill battle for survival against rising seas. As sea levels go up, wetland ecosystems suffer, saltwater contaminates aquifers, and catastrophic storms wreck coastal properties. Particularly vulnerable are low-lying lands and shallow islands. High-rise resorts perch precariously along shorelines of tiny Caribbean nations whose economies rely heavily on tourist dollars. In countries such as Bangladesh, where the flood-prone Ganges Delta is the breadbasket of the nation, the entire country—not just coastal dwellers—suffers from episodic inundation of crops. Saltwater intrusion on groundwater sources in the Marshall Islands has rendered aquifers useless. Louisiana is losing as much as 35 square miles (91 square kilometers) of wetlands a year to erosion. If sea levels continue to inch higher, the severity and frequency of the destruction will only increase.[28]*

Many of these weather changes, such as increased wildfires, storms, and flooding, will likely occur even with just 1 degree Fahrenheit (0.56 degree Celsius) of additional warming, but a greater degree of warming in the higher ranges projected by the IPCC will cause even more serious problems. As Lynn Laws of the Iowa Environmental Council explained, "More than five degrees Fahrenheit will result in up to 3.2 billion people facing water shortages, 20% of the global population affected by flooding, and 3–8 times more heat waves in some cities."[29]

Parts of the United States have already suffered from severe flooding due to climate change.

This has not only health and safety effects, but economic effects as well, as *National Geographic* mentioned. Since wealthier communities will have more resources available to fight climate change, poorer communities will be hit much harder, as will areas that are already warmer than other parts of the country. *Fast Company* magazine explained how this is all connected:

> In Phoenix, for example, where temperatures regularly reach well over 100 degrees already, an increase in average temperatures would mean an increase in deaths. Agriculture in the area would struggle with the heat and lack of rain. Workers would get less work done, especially outdoors. Energy bills would go up. In a cooler location, such as Seattle, climate change might have the opposite effect: an increase in temperatures could actually reduce mortality rates and energy costs.[30]

However, if temperatures continue to rise further, any benefit to northern areas will be temporary, and even though some areas may see a short-term benefit, the economy of the United States as a whole is expected to suffer. Additionally, northern areas will face their own challenges, such as crime rates that increase as the heat does, likely because criminals would prefer to stay home when it is cold outside. Coastal northeastern states also face the danger of flooding.

Are Polar Bears Endangered?

Some wildlife experts say one of the first results of global warming is that polar bears may go extinct. Polar bears spend much of their lives on and around floating ice sheets in the Arctic region, where they hunt for seals and raise their young. Many of these ice sheets, however, have been rapidly melting due to global warming, sometimes leaving bears stranded on open seawaters. Polar bears can swim long distances, but they may get tired and drown if they are too far from an ice platform. In addition, researchers are seeing a change in the bears' habits, with many bears choosing to stay on or near land, and a change in ocean ecosystems may mean there is less food for them to eat. However, other experts say polar bears are in less danger than people think; although some subspecies are threatened, it is unlikely they will all go extinct even if the temperature continues to rise.

Effects on Plants and Animals

The changes in the environment are expected to severely test the resilience of many plant and animal ecosystems, and they are expected to lead to mass extinctions of many species. In fact, according to an article published in *Nature* in 2004, climate change could threaten nearly 1 million land species—a quarter of the plant and animal species living today—by the year 2050. The article discussed a study of six biodiversity-rich regions around the world representing 20 percent of the earth's land area. In these regions, scientists used climate models designed to imitate the way that species' ranges might change in response to warming temperatures and climate conditions. The scientists found that 15 to 35 percent of the 1,103 plants, mammals, birds, reptiles, frogs, butterflies, and other invertebrates studied could become extinct. If this percentage is applied globally, it could mean 1 million species will go extinct due to global warming.

Meanwhile, increases in ocean temperatures will most certainly have a negative effect on the vital chain of biodiversity, the world's great variety and complexity of life-forms, that keeps the seas and their fish populations healthy. The world's precious coral systems, which provide protections and shelter to many different species of fish, could bleach, or lose their color due to environmental stress, and eventually die. The oceans are also becoming more acidic, a phenomenon that will lead to the deaths of many more marine creatures. Shellfish, sea urchins, starfish, and plankton will

Higher ocean acidity is causing coral reefs to die, which has in turn affected many other species of marine life.

be particularly affected because they may not be able to form skeletons and shells if the oceans become too acidic. The loss of plankton, a food source for many larger fish, and habitat changes caused by warmer ocean temperatures will in turn threaten other fish species, as well as large marine mammals such as whales and dolphins. In fact, a study conducted by an international team of scientists and ecologists and published in the journal *Science* in 2006 predicted that all species of wild seafood may collapse, or become depleted by 90 percent, by the year 2050 due to a combination of overfishing and climate change.

THE PROBLEM WITH CLIMATE MODELS

"In many regions different models cannot even agree on whether the climate will become wetter or drier. For example, a recent study of future flows in the River Thames at Kingston shows a possible 11% increase over the next 80 years relative to the last 60 years. However, under an identical emissions scenario, the same report shows an alternative projection of a 7% decrease in flows."

–Dr. Neil Mcintyre, Department of Civil and Environmental Engineering, and Grantham Institute for Climate Change, Imperial College London

Dr. Neil Mcintyre and Grantham Institute, Imperial College London, "How Will Climate Change Impact on Fresh Water Security?," *Guardian*, December 21, 2012. www.theguardian.com/environment/2012/nov/30/climate-change-water.

Effects on Resources

For humans, climate change may not only diminish seafood from the oceans; it also may mean declining water supplies and decreased agricultural productivity. Although some regions may experience floods and rising seas, other parts of the world will suffer from drought and reduced rainfall. With the world's population rapidly increasing, these problems could become very serious, producing widespread water shortages and more hunger and malnutrition, especially for people in less developed areas. The ways climate change affects the global water supply is complex and can be confusing. For instance, even though climate change can cause heavier rainfall in some areas, this can have mixed effects. It can help by adding to fresh water sources, but it can also harm by making that fresh water move back to the ocean more quickly, making it harder for people to store and use it. This lack of water, along with other climate changes, could cause a decline in food production, particularly in developing countries located close to the equator such as India and Sudan. As a result, the IPCC projected that by 2030, malnutrition will rise dramatically, and that by 2080, 200 million to 600 million people may not have enough food to eat.

DISASTROUS RESULTS

"The most recent international moves towards combating global warming represent a recognition ... that if the emission of greenhouse gases ... is allowed to continue unchecked, the effects will be catastrophic—on the level of nuclear war."

—International Institute for Strategic Studies (IISS), a London-based public policy and education organization that focuses on political and military issues

Quoted in Jeremy Lovell, "Global Warming Impact Like 'Nuclear War.'" Reuters, September 12, 2007. www.commondreams.org/archive/2007/09/12/3791/.

Notably, the most vulnerable agricultural crops may be grains, such as wheat, corn, and rice, the main dietary staples for much of the world's population. Experts say these crops tend to be extremely sensitive to higher temperatures, and they are already being grown in the tropics and subtropics just under the maximum temperatures they will tolerate. In 2006, the Consultative Group on International Agricultural Research, an organization representing many of the world's top crop research centers, examined the impact of climate change on wheat, the source of one-fifth of the world's food. Computer models used by researchers predicted that by 2050, warming weather conditions would ruin wheat crops in a vast, now fertile wheat-growing region that stretches from Pakistan through Northern India and Nepal to Bangladesh. This would threaten the food supply of 200 million people. Experts say other major food sources, such as cereals and corn produced in Africa and the rice crop in much of India and Southeast Asia, are at similar risk.

Like some other impacts of climate change, however, the majority of the consequences may fall on developing countries. While countries located in temperate regions, such as the continental United States and Europe, may see a small overall increase in agricultural yields due to warmer temperatures, countries in warmer climates, many of them poorer nations, will face food declines.

Wheat is one of the crops that is expected to suffer most from climate change.

Fighting for Resources

One potential effect that does not seem naturally tied to climate change is an increase in war. Studies have found that countries with a high level of ethnic tension are more likely to fight when natural disasters such as drought and heat waves occur. Additionally, experts warn that if climate change does significant damage to parts of the world, military conflicts could break out as nations compete for dwindling water, food, energy, housing, and other resources. Many military experts, in fact, see the climate crisis as a threat multiplier that will intensify global political instability by creating pressures—such as water shortages, food insecurity, disease, and flooding—on some of the world's most fragile governments.

A HUMAN PROBLEM

"[People] have trouble imagining a future drastically different from the present. We block out complex problems that lack simple solutions. We dislike delayed benefits and so are reluctant to sacrifice today for future gains. And we find it harder to confront problems that creep up on us than emergencies that hit quickly."

–Beth Gardiner, *New York Times* reporter

Beth Gardiner, "We're All Climate-Change Idiots," *New York Times*, July 21, 2012. www.nytimes.com/2012/07/22/opinion/sunday/were-all-climate-change-idiots.html?_r=0.

The Effect of Climate Change on Wildfires

In recent years, Southern California has experienced a series of wildfires that have caused significant property damage for homeowners. Whether these fires are connected to global warming has been a hotly debated topic. Experts say the answer to this question depends on whether the ongoing drought in the U.S. Southwest is related to climate change. Some researchers say the drought could, indeed, be related to climate change. They point out several factors:

- Rising temperatures dry out plants, making them more likely to catch and spread fire.

- Lightning, which occurs more often during warm weather, may be starting fires more frequently.

- Spring is coming early in many parts of the world, which makes the fire season longer.

- An increase in fires can cause positive feedback by decreasing the number of carbon-absorbing trees and increasing the amount of carbon dioxide from smoke.

Other scientists, however, downplay the connection between fires and global warming, pointing out that large wildfires are a common occurrence in Southern California. They state that the damage caused by recent wildfires is due largely to the accumulation of fuel from modern fire suppression policies and the fact that people are increasingly building homes in rural, fire-prone areas.

The press has revealed that a secret report prepared by the U.S. Department of Defense in 2004 contained an even grimmer outlook on the dangers of climate change. According to the report, the warming climate could produce famine, widespread riots, millions of homeless migrants, and a decrease in the planet's ability to sustain its current population. The report concluded that global warming is a major national security concern because climate changes will raise issues of survival that will lead many countries into wars with their neighbors. Abrupt warming, the report predicted, could even result in global anarchy—that is, lawlessness, civil disorder, and wars—because nations might use the threat of nuclear weapons to defend and secure dwindling food, water, and energy supplies. If this occurs, the report warned, "disruption and conflict will be endemic [common] features of life ... Once again, warfare would define human life."[31]

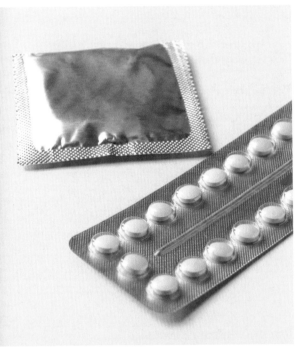

Reducing the birth rate by using birth control has been suggested as one way humanity can ensure there are enough resources to go around.

Part of the problem is that in addition to shrinking resources, the planet's population is growing. Sir David Attenborough, the presenter of BBC's documentary series *Planet Earth*, has worked with conservation organizations and come to the conclusion that an important part of the solution is for humanity to start limiting its growth. Attenborough said, "We are a plague on Earth. It's coming home to roost over the next 50 years or so. It's not just climate change; it's sheer space, places to grow food for this enormous horde."[32] He advocates for better sex education as well as increased access to affordable birth control and abortion throughout the world so the birth rate will begin to decrease.

This is just one area in which humanity needs to change to avoid catastrophe. According to experts, the technology exists; the main problem, however, is getting policy makers as well as the general public to understand that dramatic changes need to be made to most countries' current lifestyle.

Fighting Climate Change

Although many people agree on the need to take action against climate change, putting those actions into practice—and even agreeing on what those actions should be—has proven to be a challenge. One of the biggest obstacles is that most societies are currently designed to be completely dependent on non-renewable energy. Making changes in these areas can be expensive and sometimes impractical—for example, switching an entire city from electricity to solar power. This is a plan that cannot be completed in a day or even a year.

However, the use of fossil fuels goes far beyond the obvious sources. Manufacturing is one important example, especially when demand for a product is high. Creating things cheaply and quickly takes a lot of work, and most of the processes are not sustainable. Making a plastic bottle for bottled water, for instance, requires large amounts of oil, not only to create the plastic but also to power the machines in the factory. The emissions that come from manufacturing plants contribute to the greenhouse gas problem, and many people do not recycle their plastic bottles. When people throw away plastic, it never breaks down; it sits in a landfill, taking up space. Finally, plastic can leak harmful chemicals into the environment, causing further health problems for humans and animals.

Reliance on Fossil Fuels

Oil, natural gas, and coal provide the energy that heats and cools most homes and powers most cars and airplanes. Fossil fuels also provide the electricity essential to maintaining a modern lifestyle, which is dependent on computers, telephones, televisions, and numerous other machines and appliances. The world economy, too, requires cheap fossil fuels to manufacture many products, to grow food, and to transport people and products around the globe. Developed countries use the largest share of energy, while less developed nations use very little. The United States is one of the world's highest energy users.

World energy consumption is likely to grow in the future. The world population is increasing rapidly, particularly in developing countries. People in these countries want all the same technologies now available to people in developed countries. Altogether, more people with more economic wealth wanting cars, computers, and appliances means there will be an ever-increasing demand for more energy in the future. If this added energy demand is satisfied by burning fossil fuels, it will produce a significant increase in greenhouse emissions. In fact, some experts say that if people in developing countries adopt the same energy-intensive lifestyles as people in developed countries, global carbon emissions could triple—a level that most scientists believe would result in catastrophic climate change.

As more people around the world buy items such as cars and phones, the reliance on fossil fuels is likely to rise.

According to climate experts, climate change cannot be reversed at this point, but it is still possible for humans to curb the worst effects. However, in order to do so, changes need to start being put into place immediately. The 2007 IPCC report concluded that catastrophic global warming can be avoided if the world took immediate and decisive action to stabilize and then reduce greenhouse emissions. The IPCC recommended that a variety of methods be used to achieve this goal—everything from increasing energy efficiency to greater reliance on nuclear energy to development of new and emerging technologies, including renewable energy sources. The 2007 IPCC report also encouraged governments to use a wide range of political tools, such as regulations and standards, taxes, trading schemes, subsidies, financial incentives, and research and development programs. However, most of the IPCC's warnings were ignored as people, especially policy makers, continued to deny climate change. As a result, Christiana Figueres, vice-chair of the Global Covenant of Mayors for Climate and Energy, said in 2017 that the world has only three more years to act in order to make the transition to an economy based on renewable resources a smooth and effective one.

States Take Action

In the United States, the federal response to global warming has been slow. The lack of federal efforts, however, has inspired states and localities to take action. For instance, in 2006, California enacted the first mandatory and enforceable statewide program to cap carbon emissions from major industries. California's goal is to reduce total state greenhouse emissions to 1990 levels by 2020 and to reduce emissions by 80 percent by 2050. Following California's lead, 19 other states and the District of Columbia have also created specific emissions targets. Additionally, California has set a goal of having 50 percent of its electricity come from renewable sources by 2030. Many other states have committed to this as well. Five states—Idaho, Hawai'i, Maine, Delaware, and Rhode Island—as well as the District of Columbia have 100 percent of their energy coming from sources such as wind, solar, and hydro (water) power.

Pros and Cons of Renewable Energy

The ideal solution to global warming would be a technological one that allows the world to switch quickly from fossil fuels to clean, sustainable energy sources such as solar, wind, biomass, and geothermal. Clean energy sources emit zero or low levels of carbon dioxide, and sustainable sources are renewable, unlike fossil fuels, which will eventually all be used up. Each of these sources, however, has its limitations.

According to many experts, wind power is the most promising source of clean energy. Turbines capture the energy of the wind using propeller-like blades positioned on 100-foot-high

(30.5 m) towers, and the moving blades are connected to turbines to generate electricity. Supporters say even a small wind tower could produce more than half of the electricity used by an average home, but more massive wind farms could contribute a significant share to utility grids. Denmark, for example, already generates more than 40 percent of its electricity from wind and plans to reach 50 percent by 2020. However, wind energy on its own is not reliable because to work efficiently, wind turbines "need smooth, laminar airflow; the kind you only really find at about 100 meters (328 feet) above the ground."[33] Additionally, many people think large wind turbines detract from the beauty of landscapes and views. To address these problems, one company has created a wind turbine that could potentially work without blades, although its claims have yet to be proven. Another company is working on a turbine that looks like a tree so it is prettier to look at.

FOCUS LESS ON THE ECONOMY

"2020 is a hard deadline. There's no turning back if we don't bend the emissions curve within three years ... There are no jobs on a dead planet."

—Sharan Burrow, general secretary of the International Trade Union Confederation

Quoted in Kendra Pierre-Louis, "Researchers Say We Have Three Years to Act on Climate Change Before It's Too Late," *Popular Science*, June 28, 2017. www.popsci.com/three-years-to-act-on-climate-change.

Solar energy is another renewable technology. Supporters say the amount of sun energy that hits the earth every day is enormous. According to the Union of Concerned Scientists, a leading science organization, "Averaged over the entire surface of the planet, 24 hours per day for a year, each square meter [of land on Earth] collects the approximate energy equivalent of almost a barrel of oil each year, or 4.2 kilowatt-hours of energy every day."[34] The two main types of solar systems are solar hot water and photovoltaic cells. Solar water systems are generally simple boxes with liquid-filled pipes that are placed on the rooftops of buildings to absorb solar rays and heat household water. Solar photovoltaic (PV) cells, made from silicon, are a more complex type of rooftop system that can convert solar heat directly into electricity to power homes and businesses, add to a larger electrical grid, or be stored in batteries.

Countries such as Germany and Japan have already invested heavily in clean energy, and the United States may soon follow their example. California's solar plants set a record in 2016, producing 8,030 megawatts (MW) of energy—enough to power 6 million homes. In Germany in October 2017, solar and wind energy produced so much electricity that the cost was negative, so citizens actually got paid for using electricity. As the National Renewable Energy Laboratory of the U.S. Department of Energy explained, "Solar energy represents a huge domestic energy resource for the United States, particularly in the Southwest where the deserts have some of the best solar resource levels in the world. For example, an area approximately 12 percent the size of Nevada has the potential to supply all of the electric needs of the United States."[35] So far, however, solar energy systems only capture a fraction of the sun's energy, and they do not work when it is raining. For this reason, solar energy systems must be combined with backup power such as a generator—which would likely run on fossil fuels—or batteries, which can be expensive. Research is underway that could produce much more efficient and less costly solar energy systems, but solar energy's future largely depends on these technological developments.

Wind turbines such as these can help create energy, but some people do not like them because they think they are ugly.

Geothermal energy, which is generated by heat from deep inside the earth, is also a clean energy source that can be used either directly for heating buildings or indirectly for generating electricity. According to some experts, just 1 percent of the earth's geothermal energy can generate 500 times the amount of energy that exists in all the planet's gas and oil resources. However, it is currently very expensive to build a geothermal energy plant, and the places where they can be built must have specific conditions, which means it may cost a lot to transport the energy from the plant to the places it is supposed to power. Additionally, even though geothermal energy does not emit carbon dioxide, some systems may emit small amounts of sulfur dioxide, which is a toxic, smelly gas.

Each solar panel generally costs between $212 and $360, but they generate clean, cheap energy and do not cost much to maintain.

Biomass, or plant material, is another potential alternative energy source. Historically, humans have burned trees and other crops for heat energy, but today, researchers are focusing on non-combustion methods that turn biomass into gaseous, liquid, or solid fuels that can be used in power plants to generate electricity with significantly lower greenhouse emissions. Biomass also can be used to produce transportation fuels that produce fewer harmful emissions than gasoline. Two examples are biodiesel, an oil collected from plants that can power diesel engines, and ethanol, a type of alcohol produced from corn, sugar beets, or switchgrass that can be mixed with gasoline and used in most cars. The main limitation of biomass energy is that it would require large quantities of plant material and thus use huge areas of land for single-crop agriculture—an unsustainable practice that could further degrade rural environments. Farmers found out many years ago that crops need to be rotated; one year, a crop such as corn may be grown in a field, and the next year, a crop such as oats may be grown in that field instead. This is because some types of crops take nutrients out of the soil and other types replace those nutrients. With a single-crop system, the soil becomes bad for agriculture, leaving large areas of land unusable for anything.

The Role of Economics

Some of these sustainable energy sources can be put into place by individuals, such as installing solar panels on the roof of a home. When a household provides its own energy, independent of an energy company, it is called living off the grid. Some people like the idea of this because off-grid energy tends to be cleaner and cheaper, but it has some issues as well. One problem is that although energy costs tend to be lower after off-grid energy sources are installed, making a house energy independent comes with a very high up-front cost that many individuals cannot afford. For example, getting solar panels installed on a roof is very expensive: The person must buy the panels—which are not cheap—pay to have them installed, and pay for a battery or generator to power their home on days when the sun is not shining. The average cost of this process in the United States is $16,000.

Another problem is that the laws in some states make it difficult to live off the grid. Most places in the United States have property codes that homeowners must follow, and some of these forbid making unapproved changes to a house, such as building an addition. Some codes include installing solar panels in the list of forbidden changes, and people who request government approval are sometimes denied. Getting the proper licenses needed for approval may add even more to the up-front cost.

Even when the money is coming from a government rather than an individual, cost can be a barrier. State, local, and even federal governments only have so much money available, and transitioning from fossil fuels to renewable resources is often a slow, expensive process, which is why most governments are

committing to percentages over several years rather than immediately switching over. The cost to maintain sustainable energy
sources is relatively low, and most do not have the potential to
cause deadly accidents that are expensive to clean up, such as
oil spills and fires. However, as with installing solar panels on
a roof, they require large up-front costs that must come from
people's taxes, which some people object to. Additionally, the
standards for getting permits to build renewable energy plants
is sometimes confusing for companies and governments alike
because the new technology requires different standards than
the old ones people are used to.

People may also be unconvinced about switching to a new
form of energy, especially if their energy bills will increase. One
way this problem can be addressed is if governments subsidize,
or pay for part of, renewable energy. Oil and gas are currently
subsidized, so if the government were to switch to subsidizing
clean energy, the cost for those would increase and the cost for
renewable sources would decrease, allowing more people to
afford them. However, there are many complex political reasons
why this would be difficult, including oil and gas companies that

*Mining and burning coal have negative effects on the environment, but the
economies of some parts of the United States have been built around coal.*

give money to politicians to encourage them to vote to subsidize fossil fuels. The fact that many renewable energy companies are small and have fewer resources available limits their ability to compete with larger oil and gas companies.

DAMAGE CONTROL

"This ... [2007] IPCC report makes it clear that global warming is here now, and we must take swift and effective action to stave off the most severe consequences ... At this point, some warming is unavoidable, but there is a world of difference between 1 degree and 7 degrees."

–Dan Lashof, environmentalist and chief operating officer at NextGen Climate America, Inc., a climate change organization

Quoted in "Scientists' Urgent Climate Warning Underscores Need for Swift Action." NRDC, February 2, 2007. www.nrdc.org/media/2007/070202.

Some people also fear that switching to renewable energy will cause people to become unemployed as their jobs are replaced. This played a part in the 2016 presidential election, when candidate Hillary Clinton stated that she would close down coal companies in favor of clean energy. This statement lost her support in states where coal makes up a large part of the economy. Fear of unemployment causes many people to reject the transition to clean energy, but the reality is that clean energy will create more jobs than it destroys. In 2016, the solar industry employed about 200,000 more people than the coal industry, and if the industries keep growing, so will the jobs. Some residents of coal country are aware that it will be difficult for coal to make a huge comeback and boost their economy, so they are looking for other ways to make a living. According to Gwendolyn Christon, the owner of a grocery store in Isom, Kentucky, "It's not going to depend on the federal government or someone coming in to rescue us. It's going to be us going to work and doing it ourselves."[36] This is a difficult decision for many in areas where coal mining is a longstanding family tradition; as journalist Courtney Balestier wrote, "It's hard to overstate—and perhaps, to outsiders, hard to explain at all—the mental shift that this economic change represents, and the reevaluation of identity it prompts."[37]

Futuristic Research

As the threat of climate change becomes clearer, some scientists and entrepreneurs are creating products they hope will address some of the issues, rather than waiting for governments to take action. New, experimental products are announced nearly every day. Most are not available worldwide yet, but they may be in the future. Some of the most unusual solutions include:

- a skyscraper made out of wood and covered in carbon-absorbing plants

- methods of turning methane into an energy source

- extracting the bacteria from the stomach of a plastic-eating moth larva called a waxworm to help break down plastic waste

- a product that burns like coal but is made from wood and plants, making it renewable, clean, and environmentally friendly

- cutlery made out of wheat and rice flour so they can be eaten rather than thrown away like plastic cutlery

Other barriers to change include a low level of education among the workforce in places such as West Virginia and Kentucky; high rates of poverty, meaning many people cannot afford to go back to school or start a new business; and a loss of workers as people move away. However, many people are determined to save their communities by changing the economy to center around things such as car repair, tech companies, and aerospace mechanics.

Reducing Current Emissions

Several transportation technologies may also help to reduce carbon emissions. Hydrogen fuel is one of the most attractive because it can be stored and used like gasoline. Hydrogen can be easily produced from water by separating hydrogen from oxygen, but this requires energy, either from fossil fuels or renewable sources. Thus, hydrogen is only as emission-free as the energy that is used to produce it. Other obstacles to hydrogen gas are that it must be compressed or liquefied in order to fit into the size of a typical car's gasoline tank, and numerous hydrogen stations would have to be built to distribute the fuel, similar to the present-day gas station system. Overcoming these obstacles depends on achieving technological breakthroughs in the future. In addition, even if technical problems are solved, experts say changing a nation's infrastructure, or organization, to fit a new type of fuel presents a massive undertaking. Many energy experts are therefore skeptical about whether hydrogen can ever truly replace gasoline as a viable energy source.

Electric vehicles might also lower emissions, but they, too, depend on the development of renewable energies to produce clean electric power that can be stored in batteries. Many people also worry about their cars not being able to travel very far on a single charge, especially since there are few electric car charging stations across the United States. For this reason, hybrid vehicles containing both an electric battery-powered motor and a conventional gasoline engine are currently more popular than purely electric cars. However,

As of 2017, it is hard to find public car charging stations in the United States, which makes some people less likely to buy an electric car.

as technology improves, electric cars are expected to improve, and the price of a new electric car, which is currently much higher than a standard gasoline or hybrid car, is expected to drop; according to the website FleetCarma, electric cars are expected to be cheaper than conventional cars by 2022. They can be charged while someone is at home or work, their engines do not make noise, and the U.S. government currently offers tax credits for people who buy an electric car, which means they can get money back when they pay their yearly taxes.

Examining Existing Energy Sources

Because renewable technologies need further development, some experts argue that currently abundant fuel sources, such as coal and nuclear energy, may have to be relied on until better energy sources are available. Entrepreneurs therefore are re-searching ways to produce a form of clean, emission-free coal. One idea currently being researched is carbon capture and stor-age, which is just what it sounds like—a method of capturing the carbon dioxide that is produced from burning the coal and burying it deep underground so that it does not escape into the atmosphere.

Critics, however, claim that there is no such thing as clean coal and that even zero-emission coal plants will produce toxic wastes and damage the environment. Indeed, critics say clean coal will create just as much pollution as older coal plants be-cause clean coal plants take heavy metal toxins such as mercury out of the air but leave higher levels of these toxins in solid waste ash, much of which ends up polluting ordinary landfills. In short, air pollution is traded for ground pollution. In addi-tion, clean coal technology remains very expensive, so its usage may be limited in any case. As of early 2018, only one coal plant in the United States is using the carbon capture and storage method because of how expensive the equipment is to build.

Some people support nuclear energy, an energy source that currently provides 19.7 percent of America's electricity but one that has fallen out of favor because of environmental concerns. Nuclear power plants in the past have leaked radiation and caused accidents. One of the most infamous is the Chernobyl, Ukraine, disaster of 1986. Because of a flawed nuclear reac-tor design and poorly trained staff, the plant exploded, several people died, and there was a dramatic increase in the number of thyroid cancers diagnosed in the area. Nuclear power plants also pose the problem of how to dispose of the end product of nuclear fission—radioactive nuclear waste. After a nuclear power reactor melted down at the Three Mile Island, Pennsylvania, plant in 1979, the government imposed strict new regulations, which meant it cost more and took longer to build nuclear power plants. As a result of these environmental and safety issues as well as the rising cost, no nuclear power plants have been built in America since the 1970s. While many people do not like the idea of nuclear power, they also are not in favor of

Some people have suggested nuclear power as one solution to carbon emissions, but others worry about the dangers a nuclear reactor may pose.

ending its use completely, as this would increase reliance on fossil fuels even more. Some people believe nuclear plants can be operated safely and have called for more to be built, but others prefer to focus on different forms of energy.

Using Energy in Better Ways

Improving energy efficiency could also help reduce greenhouse emissions. In fact, according to the environmental group Natural Resources Defense Council, "The cheapest and fastest way to cut global warming pollution is to make things that use electricity—like appliances, industrial equipment and buildings—more energy-efficient."[38] Major home appliances such as refrigerators, washing machines, and dishwashers account for a large portion of people's monthly utility bills, and replacing them with new models—especially energy-efficient ones with an Energy Star label—can dramatically reduce the amount of electricity consumers use. Using energy-efficient and environmentally friendly, or "green," techniques to build homes and commercial buildings is another important objective. Some experts say that putting this technology in older buildings and establishing strong efficiency standards for new construction could cut energy consumption by 40 to 50 percent. The U.S. Green Building Council, a U.S. nonprofit coalition of building industry leaders, has already developed a green building rating system, called Leadership in Energy and Environmental Design, to promote energy-efficient, healthy, and green design and construction practices.

In addition, because gas-burning vehicles create much of the greenhouse gas problem, increasing gas mileage and vehicle efficiency would go a long way toward reducing global warming. Today, under the U.S. Corporate Average Fuel Economy (CAFE) regulations, all vehicles must get a certain number of miles per gallon. For cars and light trucks, the Obama administration set the CAFE standard at 54.5 miles (87.7 km) per gallon by 2025—up from the previous standard of 34.1 miles (54.9 km) per gallon—but after Trump took office, he announced that he would be reexamining this policy and possibly not enforcing it. Economic experts believe this would hurt the auto industry in the United States, causing people to buy foreign cars with better gas mileage. Some policy makers are also interested in regulating emissions from air travel, because aviation is the world's fastest-growing source of greenhouse gases and a major contributor to global warming.

START PREPARING NOW

"Because the risks [of global warming] to society and ecosystems could prove to be significant, it is prudent [wise] now to develop and implement strategies that address the risks ... [including] putting policies in place that start us on a path to reduce emissions."

–ExxonMobil

Quoted in "Key Players React to the IPCC Global Warming Report." *Christian Science Monitor*, February 8, 2007. www.csmonitor.com/2007/0208/p25s01-sten.html.

However, experts say that technology to foster efficiency, produce renewable energy, and help clean up fossil fuel emissions cannot be developed quickly enough to prevent dangerous levels of warming. For this reason, most scientists and global warming experts continue to press for meaningful global limits on greenhouse emissions.

CHAPTER 5

A Changing World

Researchers have made it clear that even if change is made immediately, the world will still be warmer than it was. This means governments need to commit to working on their infrastructure to make sure it can withstand the effects of climate change, such as stronger storms, worse flooding, and potentially even earthquakes and volcanic eruptions.

However, just because some warming is unavoidable does not mean nothing can be done. Individuals can make a big impact by choosing sustainable products, encouraging their elected officials to vote for certain laws, and making changes to their lifestyle. Although this seems logical, people sometimes resist these changes because sustainable products tend to be more expensive and because they are comfortable with the way they are already living. Making it easier for people to "go green" is one thing scientists and entrepreneurs are working on.

Making Structural Changes

For many years, global warming experts refused to embrace adaptation strategies, fearing that a discussion about adapting to global warming would give governments an excuse for not taking action to mitigate climate change. Today, most experts continue to stress that strong and immediate intervention is needed to protect future generations from global warming, but they accept that people also must begin to prepare for the consequences of the higher temperatures that now seem certain to occur in coming decades. As the IPCC's 2007 report explained, "Adaptation will be necessary to address impacts resulting from the warming which is already unavoidable due to past emissions."[39] Many commentators agree that these adaptation efforts must be made very soon, because global warming is already

happening and has been for several years. As author and environmental correspondent Mark Hertsgaard explained,

> For years, global warming was discussed in the hypothetical—a
> threat in the distant future. Now it is increasingly regarded as a
> clear, observable fact. This sudden shift means that all of us must
> start thinking about the many ways global warming will affect us,
> our loved ones, our property and our economic prospects. We must
> think—and then adapt accordingly.[40]

At the same time, as the IPCC report cautioned, "Adaptation
... cannot be a substitute for mitigation [reduction]."[41] Instead,
experts stress that both strategies—mitigation and adaptation—
must take place at the same time. During the next few decades,
therefore, governments around the globe must act to reduce
their greenhouse gas emissions significantly while also working
to strengthen systems to protect against stronger hurricanes, heat
waves, fires, droughts, rising seas, and other impacts of global
warming. Commentators warn that this challenge is necessary
even though it will require massive efforts and expenditures
in many countries. As Hertsgaard wrote, "Adaptation won't be
cheap. It won't be optional either."[42]

Experts say adaptation strategies will vary from region to
region depending on the effects that global warming has on different parts of the world. In places that receive more rainfall due
to climate changes, for example, the goal might be to build more
flood defenses and turn vulnerable, low-lying lands into nature
preserves that can be allowed to flood periodically. In coastal areas
where hurricanes and storms are expected to increase in number
and intensity, officials might need to strengthen coastal wetlands
to provide a storm buffer and make land-use decisions that keep
residents safe from intense weather. In regions that experience
more drought and more fires, governments may decide to revise
building codes or zoning laws, reevaluate water supply systems,
or add more firefighters to protect residents better against changing weather patterns. Meanwhile, regions affected by the spread of
infectious diseases may need to improve their health systems, and
countries that suffer from declining agriculture and food supplies
may need to import more of their food. The idea of adaptation is

that climate change must begin to be factored into all policy and planning decisions by individuals and their governments on local, national, and global levels.

Many countries have already begun to plan ahead for the effects of climate change. The Netherlands, which has historically struggled with flooding, is making its flood defenses even stronger. Britain, too, has doubled its spending on flood control and coast management in recent years. Other countries in Europe have also made various efforts to prepare for future climate changes. The United States, critics say, has been slow to respond, but the devastation caused by Hurricane Katrina in 2005 at least caused policy makers to begin thinking about how similar intense storms and other impacts of global warming might affect American towns and cities. The cost of cleaning up and recovering from the Katrina disaster ran into the hundreds of billions of dollars, and recent hurricanes such as Harvey and Irma have done more damage.

The Thames Barrier (shown here) is the world's second-largest movable flood barrier. It protects London from flooding if the River Thames rises.

ADAPTATION IS ESSENTIAL

"Climate change is here and now … We have to adapt."

–Ian Noble, chief scientific advisor for the Notre Dame Global Adaptation Initiative (ND-GAIN)

Quoted in Peter N. Spotts, "Time to Begin 'Adapting' to Climate Change?" *Christian Science Monitor,* February 13, 2007.

The Economic Burden

Achieving timely adaptation to climate change, however, may be the most difficult for poorer countries. Ironically, although developing countries contribute the least to global warming, they are expected to face the biggest global warming problems with the fewest financial and technical resources for combating these problems. While people in the United States and other industrialized nations will be affected by global warming in many ways, developing countries tend to be located in less temperate parts of the world, where higher temperatures are expected to cause more dramatic environmental changes. As former UN intern Sana Aftab Khan explained,

> *Reduced rainfall and prolonged droughts [in developing regions] could lead to dwindling water supplies, while subsistence agriculture, on which these countries depend heavily, will be damaged by increased tropical cyclones, droughts and loss of soil fertility. Coastal flooding, droughts and diseases could also force many people out of their homes.*[43]

An Increase in Allergens

Although global warming may help some crops and beneficial plants to grow, it also could spur the growth of harmful plants, such as those that produce allergic reactions in many people. Global warming is expected to produce higher levels of carbon dioxide in the atmosphere and warmer temperatures. In addition, this warming has caused spring to arrive earlier in many locations, leading to a longer growing period. All these conditions, researchers say, are expected to cause common plants to produce more pollen and allergens—particles that cause many people, especially those who suffer from asthma, to sneeze, itch, and have trouble breathing. According to a recent study by Duke University scientists, the amount of pollen produced by the ragweed plant—a weed common to North America that is a major source of allergic reactions—is expected to more than double if carbon emissions continue to climb in the future. Researchers say rising atmospheric levels of carbon dioxide will also likely fuel the growth of other weeds.

Also, poorer countries are less able to devote funds to infrastructure and other projects to protect against extreme weather or recover from disasters that could be caused by global warming. Americans might have to drive a smaller car or pay more for water or food, but people in poor countries may lose their homes, their jobs, their food and water, or even their lives.

Bangladesh, for example, is a poor, low-lying country of 164 million people that has already experienced higher-than-normal flooding in the last decade caused by rising sea levels believed to be a result of global warming. According to retired national meteorologist M. H. Khan Chowdhury, "On an average, river erosion takes away about [19,000 acres] of land every year … [and] about one million people are directly or indirectly affected by river-bank erosion every year in Bangladesh."[44] If sea levels rise as much as expected if no action is taken to mitigate global warming, experts predict that rising waters will cover more than 15 percent of the country, displacing more than 13 million people and seriously damaging the nation's rice fields, which provide much of its food. Today, Bangladesh is trying to raise roads, wells, and houses to higher levels and cope with rising seas but is having difficulty doing so because of insufficient resources.

Meanwhile, in the semi-arid region of Africa south of the Sahara desert, reduced rainfall may put food and water at risk and threaten the existence of people and animals alike. As Paul Desanker of the United Nations Framework Convention on Climate Change warned, "If carbon pollution is left unchecked, climate change will have a pervasive effect on life in Africa … It will threaten the people, animals and natural resources that make Africa unique."[45] Global warming could also lead to much higher rates of disease in developing parts of the world that are already struggling to contain a variety of epidemics.

Bangladesh, shown here, is at risk for increased flooding but does not have as many resources as wealthier countries to make infrastructure changes.

Because of the unequal burden of climate change, the IPCC has urged developed nations to help the developing countries cope with the changes that will be brought by global warming. In most cases, this will mean providing financial assistance to poorer countries to enable them to pay for such things as flood protection, food, and aid for those who suffer damage from weather disasters.

Going Green

For all countries, the key to adapting to climate change may be implementing sustainable development—a term defined by the World Commission on Environment and Development as "development that meets the needs of the present without compromising the ability of future generations to meet their own needs."[46] Long before today's concerns about global warming, advocates for sustainable development argued that human activities were exploiting environmental treasures and ecosystems at an unsustainable rate that would eventually destroy the planet. In 1894, a report by the State Fish and Game Commissioner of North Dakota commented,

> *Present needs and present gains was the rule of action—which seems to be a sort of transmitted quality which we in our now enlightened time have not wholly outgrown, for even now a few men can be found who seem willing to destroy the last tree, the last fish and the last game bird and animal, and leave nothing for posterity [future generations], if thereby some money can be made.*[47]

This irresponsible use of natural resources, many environmentalists have claimed, has not only caused serious environmental destruction, but also deepening poverty and inequality for people in many developing regions of the world. Advocates have long urged governments around the world to embrace sustainable development as a way to repair this damage and avoid environmental and human catastrophe.

Today, experts say global warming and related climate changes are adding significantly to the stresses on the environment. Many commentators, including the IPCC, have therefore renewed the call for sustainable development as a way to ease the earth's vulnerability to climate change. As the IPCC explained in its 2007 report, by reducing pollution and overdevelopment, sustainable development could help increase the environment's ability to rebound from higher temperatures and related climate impacts.

A large part of the problem, however, is that today's economic systems do not measure pollution or other environmental impacts or include them in the costs of products produced from natural resources. Instead, these environmental costs are passed along to society in the form of health problems, environmental cleanup, and other expenses. For example, airlines do not pay for the large amounts of carbon dioxide they put into the atmosphere, and the price of food does not reflect the costs of water, air, and soil pollution caused by the runoff of chemical pesticides and fertilizers used in modern agriculture. Moving to a sustainable development model, therefore, will involve making fundamental changes in the way the world economy works—a major undertaking for all nations.

The Role of the Government

One of the fears people have about fighting climate change is that it will have a negative effect on the economy of the world as well as individual countries. Reducing greenhouse emissions, some say, will add to the normal costs of doing business and slow the economies of many nations around the world. In the United States, President Trump has been vocal about these concerns, stating that if companies are expected to make changes to cut their emissions and avoid polluting the areas around them, their expenses will rise and they will be unable to compete with foreign companies. As a result, he has repealed many of the Obama administration's climate policies. One government spokesperson said, "I think the president has been very clear that he is not going to pursue climate change policies that put the U.S. economy at risk. It is very simple."[48]

While many of Trump's supporters applaud his decisions, a larger number of people—including climatologists and business experts—have criticized his actions. Journalist Andrew Winston wrote in the *Harvard Business Review*, "These backward-looking policies will damage our economy, place us well behind other major economies, and put the planet at risk (a planet, by the way, that supports the economy and society, not the other way around)."[49]

Economists have known for years that the costs of unchecked climate change will be staggering, even in the United States. In 2007, a study by University of Maryland researcher Matthias Ruth found that climate impacts will be widespread, affecting various sectors of the economy, such as rising water costs for agriculture; added infrastructure costs for building and maintaining water and sewer facilities; increased energy costs for more summer cooling; higher health care bills; and repairing property damage caused by storms, fires, and rising seas. As Ruth explained, "Climate change will affect every American economically in significant, dramatic ways, and the longer it takes to respond, the greater the damage and the higher the costs."[50] In fact, going green is expected to create many new jobs, including some that have not been seen before. These include urban rooftop farmers, water quality technicians, clean car engineers, recycling facility workers, green builders and architects, solar cell technicians, and clean energy workers.

Oil spills cause a lot of damage and are expensive to clean up.

Trump was the nominee of the Republican party, which generally opposes government involvement in people's private lives and businesses. For this reason, many of his supporters believe less government regulation is a good thing. However, Trump's economic policies have sparked outrage and resistance among people who believe government involvement is necessary to make businesses take actions that benefit the environment, especially if it is cheaper or easier for them to do something that harms the environment. *National Geographic* created a continuously-updated article detailing the actions his administration has taken and why they can be seen as harmful to the environment. As of November 2017,

- The Dakota Access and Keystone XL oil pipelines were approved. In November 2017, less than a year after its approval, the Keystone XL pipeline leaked 210,000 gallons (794,936.5 L) of oil in South Dakota. Oil spills, both on land and in the ocean, cause widespread damage to plants, animals, and humans and are difficult and expensive to clean up. Native Americans are disproportionately affected, as the pipelines often run through reservation lands.

- ExxonMobil CEO Rex Tillerson was appointed to the post of secretary of state, which many say represents a conflict of interest—Tillerson may be more likely to favor policies and international agreements that benefit oil companies rather than companies that produce clean energy.

- Several Obama-era environmental protections were repealed, and a repeal was proposed on several more. These include the Stream Protection Rule, which "placed stricter restrictions on dumping mining waste into surrounding waterways,"[51] and the Clean Power Plan, which aimed to reduce emissions.

- Scott Pruitt, a vocal climate change denier who has opposed past Environmental Protection Agency (EPA) regulations, was appointed as the head of the EPA.

- A ban on the use of lead ammunition in hunting was repealed, which concerned critics who say lead bullets can poison other wildlife as well as hunters.

- The EPA decided not to track the emissions of oil and natural gas companies.

- Large cuts were made to the budgets of science and environmental agencies such as the EPA and the National Oceanic and Atmospheric Administration (NOAA).

- Against the advice of the EPA's chemical safety experts, Pruitt decided not to ban the use of a pesticide called chlorpyrifos, which has been linked to brain damage in children and farmworkers.

- Trump reviewed about 40 protected national monuments to see if any should be unprotected and used for economic gain.

- Offshore oil and gas drilling was expanded, which critics say can be deadly for marine life.

- Protections on certain animals were reviewed to see if they could be hunted.

- A rule protecting whales from becoming entangled in fishing nets was done away with.

- Trump signed an executive order repealing "federal flood-risk standards that incorporated rising sea levels predicted by climate science."[52] Trump's supporters say this will improve business by making the environmental review process for infrastructure changes quicker and cheaper, while opponents say it will put towns at increased risk for flooding.

- A study into the health risks of coal mining was suspended.

- A federal climate advisory panel was disbanded.

- Trump decided to pull out of the Paris Climate Agreement, making the United States the only country to oppose it.

These are only a few of the actions reported by *National Geographic*. Trump and his supporters say these actions will improve the economy in the United States, while his opponents say that in addition to harming the environment, many will actually make the economy worse. If other countries continue to commit to using sustainable power, they are unlikely to want to buy unsustainable products from the United States.

Government employees who are concerned about the Trump administration's official position on climate change have created rogue, or unofficial, Twitter accounts, tweeting information from scientists and other experts who support action on climate change. The first to be created was AltUSNatParkService, followed by Rogue NASA, AltUSForestService, U.S. EPA—Ungagged, and many more.

Many experts say environmentally friendly laws can be passed that do not hurt the economy. As the UN Foundation explained in a February 2007 report,

Significant harm from climate change is already occurring, and further damages are a certainty. The challenge now is to keep climate change from becoming a catastrophe. There is still a good chance of succeeding in this, and of doing so by means that create economic opportunities that are greater than the costs and that advance rather than impede other societal goals.[53]

The March for Science

In April 2017, thousands of scientists as well as people who support scientific research and oppose the Trump administration's policies concerning climate change marched on Washington, D.C., to show the administration that they support continued government-funded scientific research of all kinds—addressing not just climate change concerns, but anti-vaccination claims and the problems with the water supply in Flint, Michigan, which is undrinkable because of the amount of lead and other toxins in it. The event sparked hundreds of similar rallies across the United States as well as in other countries.

Like the January 2017 Women's March on Washington, D.C., the March for Science was not without controversy; for instance, organizers of both marches faced accusations that they had excluded people of color. Many hope that future protests will be more inclusive.

Science supporters marched on Washington, D.C., to show the Trump administration that they want scientific research of all kinds to continue.

Change Starts at Home

Although action by national governments and global alliances will be necessary to make the fundamental economic and other changes needed to adapt to temperature increases and shift away from fossil fuels, individuals can also play a role. They can try to reduce their own personal carbon production, called their "carbon footprint," and make plans to live with warmer temperatures and other expected climate changes.

Some people do not want to change their lifestyle at all, while others like the idea of going green but do not put it into practice for various reasons. Reading blogs or seeing news items about people who live a "zero-waste" lifestyle can be overwhelming and intimidating, not to mention expensive to put into practice. Some people believe their actions will not make a difference one way or another; although it is true that one person does not make much of a difference, the combined effort of millions of people would create an enormous change. Some feel discouraged because they cannot see the direct results of their efforts, some are too busy to make large changes in their lifestyle, and some believe it is simply too much work.

Many people are so used to the amount of packaging that comes with a modern lifestyle that they no longer notice it.

The most extreme form of sustainable lifestyle is called a zero-waste lifestyle. This is very difficult for many people to achieve because of the amount of waste and unsustainable products that are part of a normal lifestyle for most people. For instance, simply buying things at the grocery store generates waste—nearly everything is in packaging, and most of this is never recycled. This results in overfilled landfills and trash where it should not be, such as in the ocean and on beaches, which poses a danger to wildlife. People who live a zero-waste lifestyle do things such as bringing their own jars to the grocery store and their own mugs to the coffee shop, avoiding products that come in packages, recycling whenever possible, and making their own products such as bandages and shampoo.

Society's emphasis on convenience and disposability has made it stressful and expensive for many people to switch to a zero-waste lifestyle. For example, many women use disposable menstrual pads or tampons when their period begins. Before these were invented, women used rags that they rinsed out. The invention of disposable items was considered a great achievement; today, many women are disgusted by the idea of keeping a used sanitary item and find carrying around a disposable item to be more convenient. However, in recent years, some women have decided to switch back to reusable items. These have both good and bad aspects. They cost more up front—a Diva Cup, a popular hygiene product that can be inserted like a tampon, costs about $30 as of 2017, and reusable pads also cost significantly more than a package of disposable ones—but they last longer and save women money in the long run. Women who do not have the extra money, however, may not be able to make the switch. This is another example of how poor people are disproportionately affected by problems with sustainability. Reusable sanitary items must also be rinsed out, which some women do not want to do, but those who have tried these items say it does not take long to get used to doing it.

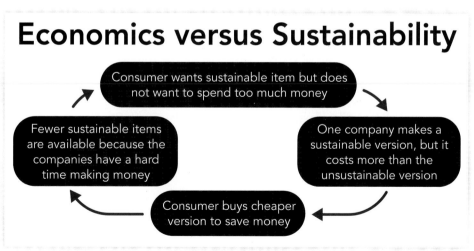

Economics versus Sustainability

Consumer wants sustainable item but does not want to spend too much money

One company makes a sustainable version, but it costs more than the unsustainable version

Consumer buys cheaper version to save money

Fewer sustainable items are available because the companies have a hard time making money

Many people do not realize that when they choose to save money in the short term, it encourages companies to keep using unsustainable manufacturing practices to keep their costs down.

It is important to note that change can begin small, and people can start by choosing the easiest things. For example, people can try to travel less. Air travel burns more fossil fuel per person than any other mode of transportation, so avoiding flying can significantly reduce contributions to emissions. Private automobiles are the second-biggest offenders in creating carbon emissions, so driving less, riding a bike, carpooling, or using public transportation when possible is another way to help reduce global warming. Buying an electric car can help as well; however, as previously noted, these are currently more expensive than standard cars, and some people may not be able to afford them. Additionally, in some places, public transportation is difficult to use or nonexistent, and weather conditions or the distance of the destination sometimes prevents people from riding their bikes. These are things that may cause people to get discouraged about living a sustainable lifestyle; some people try to make too many changes at once and get overwhelmed or believe that if they cannot make one change, they should not bother making any. However, even small changes, such as driving one day less per week, can be helpful. People should focus on doing what they can.

Home heating and cooling is the next biggest source of carbon emissions. Using sweaters and blankets in the winter, setting thermostats slightly lower, and using fans and opening windows for summer cooling can help address this problem. Insulating homes can also help reduce both heating and cooling costs. Another simple way to reduce home emissions is reducing electricity usage by buying more efficient appliances and using more efficient lighting options. Consumers can look for the blue Energy Star labels, which signify energy efficiency, and substitute compact fluorescent bulbs for incandescent ones. In fact, according to the EPA, if every American household replaced one of their most-used light bulbs with a compact fluorescent light bulb, it would be the equivalent of removing 800,000 cars and save enough energy each year to light 3 million homes. Even better, homeowners can use light-emitting diode (LED) light bulbs, which will last 50,000 hours, or around 11 to 17 years, but consume only about 10 percent of the electricity used by incandescent bulbs. Home electric usage can also be reduced by simply unplugging computers, televisions, and appliances when they are not in use. Even if they are turned off, experts say, many electronic devices continue to use energy as long as they are plugged into an electric outlet.

Finally, when planning for the future, individuals can incorporate climate change into their decision-making. For example, plastic is a big problem because of the oil needed to create it and the fact that it does not biodegrade, or break down, after it is thrown away. However, plastic makes up so many items that people use regularly that it is difficult to imagine how society could get along without it. Recycling it is a good start, but this still requires fossil fuels. For this reason, many companies are looking into replacement materials, including plastics made out of organic material that biodegrades completely.

Other choices individuals can make include:

- buying more locally produced food

- growing a home vegetable garden

- composting waste instead of throwing it away

- eating less meat

- buying secondhand clothing and recycling or mending old clothes instead of throwing them out—the creation of new clothes currently accounts for about 3 percent of all carbon emissions

- using silverware instead of plastic cutlery

- bringing a reusable bag to stores instead of taking a plastic bag

- wrapping gifts in recyclable paper or cloth

- drying clothes outdoors when the weather is nice or indoors on a drying rack

- asking not to be given a straw at restaurants

- using reusable cloths instead of paper towels or paper napkins

- reusing items when possible; for instance, using both sides of a sheet of paper before recycling it

- taking classes that teach people how to cook, garden, or make other sustainable changes

- taking shorter showers

Small changes, such as planting a home garden or switching to more efficient light bulbs, are ways individuals can take action against climate change.

Citizens can also let their concerns about climate change be known to their governments. As the environmental group Natural Resources Defense Council said,

> *We need new laws that will steer our nation toward the most important solutions to global warming—cleaner cars and cleaner power plants. Send a message to your elected officials, letting them know that you will hold them accountable for what they do—or fail to do—about global warming.*[54]

All of these types of individual choices, multiplied by the millions of people in the United States and billions more in the rest of the world, can have a tremendous effect on the planet's future.

Introduction: Ignored for Too Long

1. "Al Gore—Nobel Lecture," Nobelprize.org, December 10, 2007. www. nobelprize.org/nobel_prizes/peace/laureates/2007/gore-lecture_en.html.

Chapter 1: Understanding Climate Change

2. John P. Rafferty and Stephen P. Jackson, "Little Ice Age (LIA)," *Encyclopedia Britannica*, accessed November 7, 2017. www.britannica. com/science/Little-Ice-Age.

3. Mayer Hillman, Tina Fawcett, and Sudhir Chella Rajan, *The Suicidal Planet*. New York, NY: St. Martin's, 2007, p. 12.

4. Hillman, Fawcett, and Rajan, *The Suicidal Planet*, p. 15.

5. Bill Bryson, *At Home: A Short History of Private Life*. New York, NY: Doubleday, 2010, p. 214.

6. J. T. Houghton, G. J. Jenkins, and J. J. Ephraums, eds., *Climate Change: The IPCC Scientific Assessment*. Cambridge, UK: Cambridge University Press, 1990, p. xi. www.ipcc.ch/ipccreports/far/wg_I/ipcc_far_wg_I_full_report.pdf.

7. Intergovernmental Panel on Climate Change, *IPCC Second Assessment: Climate Change 1995*, December 1995, p. 5. www.ipcc.ch/pdf/climate-changes-1995/ipcc-2nd-assessment/2nd-assessment-en.pdf.

8. "Climate Change 2001: Synthesis Report," IPCC, accessed December 4, 2017. www.ipcc.ch/ipccreports/tar/vol4/index.php?idp=22.

9. Core Writing Team, Rajendra K. Pachauri, Andy Reisinger, eds., *Climate Change 2007: Synthesis Report*, Sweden, 2008. www.ipcc.ch/pdf/assessment-report/ar4/syr/ar4_syr_full_report.pdf.

10. Naomi Oreskes, "Beyond the Ivory Tower: The Scientific Consensus on Climate Change," *Science*, December 3, 2004, p. 1,686. www.sciencemag.org/cgi/content/full/306/5702/1686.

11. Quoted in Gregory T. Haugan, *The New Triple Constraints for Sustainable Projects, Programs, and Portfolios*. Boca Raton, FL: CRC Press, 2013, p. 340.

12. Chris Mooney, "The Hockey Stick: The Most Controversial Chart in Science, Explained," *The Atlantic*, May 10, 2013. www.theatlantic.com/technology/archive/2013/05/the-hockey-stick-the-most-controversial-chart-in-science-explained/275753/.

13. Michael D. Lemonick, "So-Called Medieval Warm Period Not So Warm After All," Climate Central, October 1, 2012. www.climatecentral.org/news/so-called-medieval-warm-period-not-so-warm-15064.

14. Kate Ramsayer, "Antarctic Sea Ice Reaches New Record Maximum," NASA, October 7, 2014. www.nasa.gov/content/goddard/antarctic-sea-ice-reaches-new-record-maximum.

15. Donald Trump (@realDonaldTrump), Twitter, November 6, 2012, 11:15 a.m. twitter.com/realdonaldtrump/status/265895292191248385?lang=en.

16. Marcelo Gleiser, "ExxonMobil vs. the World," NPR, November 30, 2016. www.npr.org/sections/13.7/2016/11/30/503825417/exxonmobil-vs-the-world.

Chapter 2: The Uncertainty of the Future

17. "How Is Today's Warming Different from the Past?," NASA Earth Observatory, accessed November 14, 2017. earthobservatory.nasa.gov/Features/GlobalWarming/page3.php.

18. Annie Sneed, "Was the Extreme 2017 Hurricane Season Driven by Climate Change?," *Scientific American*, October 26, 2017. www.scientificamerican.com/article/was-the-extreme-2017-hurricane-season-driven-by-climate-change/.

19. "Irma: A Hurricane for the History Books," CNN, accessed November 14, 2017. www.cnn.com/specials/hurricane-irma.

20. Quoted in Michael Barnard, "What We Know (and Don't Know) About Climate Change," *Forbes*, August 1, 2017. www.forbes.com/sites/quora/2017/08/01/what-we-know-and-dont-know-about-climate-change/#81c0de825132.

21. Robert Talbot, "Methane Is a Powerful Greenhouse Gas, but Where Does It Come From?," *Forbes*, September 29, 2017. www.forbes.com/sites/uhenergy/2017/09/29/methane-is-a-powerful-greenhouse-gas-but-where-does-it-come-from/#2ad123595912.

22. Quoted in Elizabeth Svoboda, "Global Warming Feedback Loop Caused by Methane, Scientists Say," *National Geographic News*, August 29, 2006. news.nationalgeographic.com/news/2006/08/060829-methane-warming.html.

Chapter 3: The Dangers of Climate Change

23. Timothy Egan, "Alaska, No Longer So Frigid, Starts to Crack, Burn, and Sag," *New York Times*, June 16, 2002. www.nytimes.com/2002/06/16/us/alaska-no-longer-so-frigid-starts-to-crack-burn-and-sag.html.

24. Quoted in Associated Press, "Severe Dengue Fever Outbreak Hits Asia," NBC News, October 26, 2007. www.nbcnews.com/id/21492929/ns/health-infectious_diseases/t/severe-dengue-fever-outbreak-hits-asia/#.WiWz262ZNBw.

25. Quoted in American Society for Microbiology, "Scientists Concerned About Effects of Global Warming on Infectious Diseases," *Science Daily*, May 23, 2007. www.sciencedaily.com/releases/2007/05/070522082450.htm.

26. Core Writing Team, Pachauri, Reisinger, eds., *Climate Change 2007: Synthesis Report*.

27. Bill Bryson, *A Short History of Nearly Everything*. New York, NY: Broadway Books, 2003, "Ice Time."

28. Eileen Yam, "Earth Pulse: If You Feel Like Your Favorite Beach Keeps Getting Skimpier Each Time You Visit, It's Not Your Imagination," *National Geographic*, 2001. www.nationalgeographic.com/ngm/0102/earthpulse/.

29. Lynn Laws, "Climate Change Affects Iowans; Iowans Can Help Turn It Around," Iowa Environment Council, April 6, 2007. www.iaenvironment.org/documents/IPCCrept4-6-07.pdf.

30. Adele Peters, "This Map Shows Which Parts of the U.S. Will Suffer Most from Climate Change," *Fast Company*, June 29, 2017. www.fastcompany.com/40435889/this-map-shows-which-parts-of-the-u-s-will-suffer-most-from-climate-change.

31. Quoted in Mark Townsend and Paul Harris, "Now the Pentagon Tells Bush: Climate Change Will Destroy Us," *Observer/UK*, February 22, 2004. www.commondreams.org/headlines04/0222-01.htm.

32. Quoted in Josh Hrala, "David Attenborough Has an Important Warning About Human Population," *Science Alert*, November 11, 2016. www.sciencealert.com/the-time-david-attenborough-said-humans-are-a-plague.

Chapter 4: Fighting Climate Change

33. "New Wind Turbine Generates Electricity Without Rotating Blades," IFLScience, accessed November 16, 2017. www.iflscience.com/technology/new-bladeless-wind-turbine-looks-asparagus/.

34. Quoted in J. S. McDougall, "America Braces for Highest Heating Costs Ever," *Huffington Post*, July 17, 2008. www.huffingtonpost.com/js-mcdougall/america-braces-for-highes_b_111705.html.

35. Quoted in Bernie Sanders, "Global Warming Is Reversible," *Nation*, November 27, 2007. www.thenation.com/article/global-warming-reversible/.

36. Quoted in Courtney Balestier, "Coal Is Dying—Coal Country Doesn't Have To: Creating the Post-Coal Economy in Appalachia," *Fast Company*, December 12, 2016. www.fastcompany.com/3065766/coal-is-dying-coal-country-doesnt-have-to-creating-the-post-coal-economy-in-appalachia.

37. Balestier, "Coal Is Dying."

38. Natural Resources Defense Council, "Solving Global Warming: It Can Be Done." www.nrdc.org/globalWarming/solutions/step1.asp.

Chapter 5: A Changing World

39. "Current Knowledge About Responding to Climate Change," IPCC, accessed December 5, 2017. www.ipcc.ch/publications_and_data/ar4/wg2/en/spmsspm-d.html.

40. Mark Hertsgaard, "On the Front Lines of Climate Change," *TIME*, March 29, 2007. content.time.com/time/magazine/article/0,9171,1604879,00. html.

41. Lord Deben, "IPCC Report Highlights the Importance of Carbon Targets," *Guardian*, April 1, 2014. www.theguardian.com/ environment/2014/apr/01/ipcc-report-carbon-targets.

42. Hertsgaard, "On the Front Lines of Climate Change."

43. Sana Aftab Khan, "Saving Least Developed Countries from Disastrous Effects of Climate Change," *UN Chronicle*, July 9, 2007. www.un.org/ Pubs/chronicle/2007/webArticles/070907_LDCs_climate_change.htm.

44. Quoted in "Bangladesh Report," World View of Global Warming, accessed December 5, 2017. www.worldviewofglobalwarming.org/ pages/bangladeshreport.php.

45. Quoted in "Global Warming Threatens Africa," BBC News, August 20, 2002. news.bbc.co.uk/1/hi/world/africa/2204756.stm.

46. Quoted in Anup Shah, "Sustainable Development Introduction," Global Issues, May26,2005.www.globalissues.org/TradeRelated/Development/ Intro.asp.

47. Quoted in "When the Last Tree Is Cut Down, the Last Fish Eaten, and the Last Stream Poisoned, You Will Realize That You Cannot Eat Money," Quote Investigator, October 20, 2011. quoteinvestigator. com/2011/10/20/last-tree-cut/.

48. Quoted in Andrew Winston, "Trump's Climate Rollback Will Hurt the Economy, Not Help It," *Harvard Business Review*, March 29, 2017. hbr.org/2017/03/trumps-climate-rollback-will-hurt-the-economy-not-help-it.

49. Winston, "Trump's Climate Rollback."

50. Quoted in "Hidden Costs of Climate Change in US: Major, Nationwide, Uncounted," *Science Daily*, October 17, 2007. www.sciencedaily.com/ releases/2007/10/071017085305.htm.

51. Michael Greshko, Laura Parker, and Brian Clark Howard, "A Running List of How Trump Is Changing the Environment," *National Geographic*, October 25, 2017. news.nationalgeographic.com/2017/03/how-trump-is-changing-science-environment/.

52. Greshko, Parker, and Howard, "A Running List."

53. Rosina Bierbaum, John P. Holdren, Michael MacCracken et al., "Confronting Climate Change: Avoiding the Unmanageable and Managing the Unavoidable," Sigma Xi, February 2007, p. 1. www.sigmaxi.org/docs/default-source/Programs-Documents/Critical-Issues-in-Science/executive-summary-of-confronting-climate-change. pdf?sfvrsn=0.

54. "How to Fight Global Warming," Natural Resources Defense Council, December 18, 2003. www.nrdc.org/globalwarming/gsteps.asp.

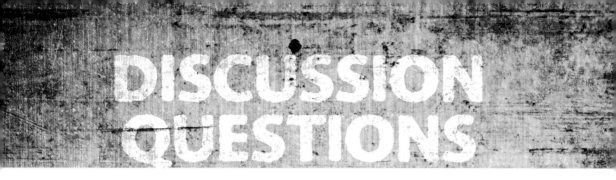

DISCUSSION QUESTIONS

Chapter 1: Understanding Climate Change

1. What is the greenhouse effect, and what role does it play in global warming? How is the greenhouse effect related to fossil fuels such as oil, coal, and natural gas?

2. What is the position of the Intergovernmental Panel on Climate Change (IPCC) on whether humans are causing climate change?

3. Do you believe in climate change? Why or why not?

Chapter 2: The Uncertainty of the Future

1. Why is it hard for researchers to accurately predict how the climate will change?

2. Why is climate change happening faster than expected?

3. Give some examples of positive and negative climate feedbacks that may affect future global warming. Can you think of any that were not mentioned in the book?

Chapter 3: The Dangers of Climate Change

1. What are some of the current effects of rising global temperatures?

2. Describe some of the possible impacts of future global warming if nothing is done to decrease emissions.

3. Describe one effect of climate change that might cause a chain of problems.

Chapter 4: Fighting Climate Change

1. Do IPCC scientists believe there is still time to avert a global warming catastrophe?

2. What are some changes you can make to help the environment?

3. What are some ways governments can decrease their countries' emissions?

Chapter 5: A Changing World

1. What types of actions can countries take to adapt to coming climate changes?

2. How will life change for individuals in the future because of climate change?

3. After reading this book, do you now have a different opinion on climate change, or has it stayed the same?

ORGANIZATIONS TO CONTACT

iMatter Youth
(952) 715-7535
info@imatteryouth.org
www.imatteryouth.org

Founded in 2007 by then–13-year-old Alec Loorz and his mother, Victoria Loorz, this organization aims to get kids and young adults involved in the fight against climate change.

Mission2020
andrew.higham@mission2020.global
www.mission2020.global

This organization is committed to finding ways to reduce global emissions by 2020.

National Wildlife Federation
P.O. Box 1583
Merrifield, VA 22116
(800) 822-9919
www.nwf.org

The National Wildlife Federation is an organization that seeks to inspire Americans to protect wildlife.

Natural Resources Defense Council (NRDC)

40 West 20th Street, 11th Floor

New York, NY 10011

(212) 727-2700

www.nrdc.org

nrdcinfo@nrdc.org

> The NRDC is an environmental action organization that seeks
> to protect the planet's wildlife and to ensure a safe and healthy
> environment for all living things. Its website contains a special
> section that details the current administration's policies on
> climate change.

The Sierra Club

2101 Webster Street, Suite 1300

Oakland, CA 94612

(415) 977-5500

information@sierraclub.org

www.sierraclub.org/globalwarming/

> The Sierra Club is a well-known grassroots environmental
> organization based in the United States and founded in 1892
> by environmentalist John Muir. The group's website contains a
> section called Compass that provides general information about
> climate change as well as legislative updates, news, and articles
> on related topics such as clean energy.

Books

Fleischman, Paul. *Eyes Wide Open: Going Behind the Environmental Headlines.* Somerville, MA: Candlewick Press, 2014.

> Most of the inventions that society relies on to run smoothly were not created with the environment in mind, and many people are resistant to change. This book discusses some of the things that would need to be altered to improve the climate change crisis and why people support or oppose them.

Gore, Al. *An Inconvenient Truth: The Crisis of Global Warming.* New York, NY: Viking, 2007.

> Former vice president Gore's bestselling book about global warming has been adapted for a young adult audience. Gore's book details which human actions have aided in the destruction of the environment and what will happen if no actions are taken to fight it.

Hirsch, Rebecca. *Climate Migrants: On the Move in a Warming World.* Minneapolis, MN: Twenty-First Century Books, 2017.

> Climate change has already forced some groups of people to abandon the places they have lived for generations, and if the global warming trend continues, it may affect thousands more people. Hirsch's book examines the challenges and economic costs of relocating so many people due to climate change.

Hunter, Nick. *Science vs. Climate Change.* London, UK: Raintree, 2016.

> Scientists have come up with some incredible inventions to fight climate change, including new forms of transportation and alternative energy sources. This book discusses how climate change is affecting the earth and examines scientists' solutions.

Royston, Angela. *The Race to Survive Climate Change.* New York, NY: Rosen Publishing Group, 2015.

> This book discusses what is causing climate change as well as the effects it has on the environment.

Websites

"Climate Change 2014 Impacts, Adaptation, and Vulnerability: Summary for Policymakers"
www.ipcc.ch/pdf/assessment-report/ar5/wg2/ar5_wgII_spm_en.pdf
> This document, which summarizes the findings of the IPCC's fifth assessment in a way non-scientists can understand, gives the most recent data and recommendations on climate change.

"Short Answers to Hard Questions About Climate Change"
www.nytimes.com/interactive/2015/11/28/science/what-is-climate-change.html
> This *New York Times* article gives a good overview of the most frequently asked questions regarding climate change in easy-to-understand language.

Surging Seas
sealevel.climatecentral.org
> This interactive map by Climate Central shows how the current U.S. coastline is expected to change if the worst-case predictions of flooding come true.

350
350.org
> This nonprofit organization is dedicated to replacing fossil fuels with 100 percent renewable resources.

Union of Concerned Scientists
www.ucsusa.org
> This science-based nonprofit organization offers information about climate change, including the effects of clean energy, clean vehicles, and global warming.

U.S. Environmental Protection Agency
www.epa.gov
> This website provides information about the Trump administration's environmental policies. Since some parts of the website have not yet been updated, a link is included to the website as it looked under the Obama administration.

U.S. EPA—Ungagged
twitter.com/ungaggedepa
> In response to the Trump administration's stance on climate change, several anonymous former and current members of the EPA have created a Twitter account to share important information with the American public.

INDEX

PICTURE CREDITS

Cover (left) Bernhard Staehli/Shutterstock.com; cover (right) hramovnick/Shutterstock.com; p. 7 courtesy of NASA; p. 8 Matthias Nareyek/Getty Images for Paramount Pictures; p. 11 xkcd: 4.5 Degrees/xkcd.com/1379/; p. 13 © CORBIS/Corbis via Getty Images; p. 14 kavram/Shutterstock.com; p. 16 Everett Historical/Shutterstock.com; p. 18 Photos.com/Thinkstock; p. 19 ttsz/iStock/Thinkstock; p. 22 Freya Ingrid Morales/Anadolu Agency/Getty Images; p. 28 Sergey 402/Shutterstock.com; p. 37 lavizzara/Shutterstock.com; p. 39 troutnut/iStock/Thinkstock; p. 42 JUNGE, HEIKO/AFP/Getty Images; p. 43 iascic/Shutterstock.com; p. 44 Matt Berger/Shutterstock.com; p. 47 Rich Carey/Shutterstock.com; p. 49 Zastolskiy Victor/Shutterstock.com; p. 51 Ulet Ifansasti/Getty Images; p. 53 Kena Betancur/VIEWpress/Corbis via Getty Images; p. 55 SARAWUT KUNDEJ/Shutterstock.com; p. 58 Andrey Kozachenko/Shutterstock.com; p. 60 © istockphoto.com/belchonock; p. 62 ozanuysal/Shutterstock.com; p. 65 Fotokon/Shutterstock.com; p. 66 Patrick Civello/Shutterstock.com; p. 68 Luke Sharrett/Bloomberg via Getty Images; p. 71 RossHelen/Shutterstock.com; p. 73 mamahoohooba/Shutterstock.com; p. 77 Marc Pinter/Shutterstock.com; p. 79 Sk Hasan Ali/Shutterstock.com; p. 82 Danny E Hooks/Shutterstock.com; p. 85 bakdc/Shutterstock.com; p. 86 06photo/Shutterstock.com; p. 90 (left) Jackie McNeel/Shutterstock.com; p. 90 (right) Mile Atanasov/Shutterstock.com.

ABOUT THE AUTHOR

Anna Collins lives in Buffalo, NY, with her dog, Fitzgerald, and her husband, Jason, whom she met on a road trip across the United States. She loves coffee and refuses to write without having a full pot ready.